ARE YOU READY?

A GUIDE TO BE THE BEST VERSION OF YOU

Jackie Cantoni

Published by Realizing Dreams

Punta Gorda, Florida

ISBN 978-0-9903128-9-5

Library of Congress Control Number: 2019903037

To Jim, for sharing our journey as best friends,
James, for your continuous gift of laughter,
Nathan, for your contagious giggles,
Mom, Dad, and Diane, for making me feel like a swan.

"People will forget what you said, people will forget what you did, but people will never forget how you made them feel."
— Maya Angelou

CONTENTS

Part One

Believe in You . . . Love Being You

Part Two

Discovering You

Part Three

You Matter . . . Make Yourself a Priority

Part Four

Be Positively Contagious

Part Five
HOW to Get There

Part Six
The Whole You
Your Purpose and Brand

Part Seven
Bringing It All Together for Your Best Self

Great leaders have inspired me, throughout my life, to strive and be a better version of myself. I thank them for their motivational words and want to pass on my inspirational life lessons to you.

Sometimes, we all need the next nudge.

JC

Do You. Be You. Celebrate You.

Let go of competitive energy and refocus on success for you.
Make yourself a priority. Re-energize and rejuvenate you.
Discover your true purpose. Release negative self-chatter.
Be positively contagious. Have more courage.
Share your voice and uniqueness.
Let your personal brand shine.
Believe in you. Celebrate you.
Sparkle with self-confidence.
Choose your best self.
Follow your passion.
You Got This!
Be You.

Jackie Cantoni

Your Journey to The Best Version of YOU

Welcome!

Congratulations for taking the first step . . . on your journey to becoming the best version of you.

Are You Ready? guides you to be your personal best. This may be the little nudge you have been waiting for . . .

Let's re-energize and rejuvenate YOU.

Part One: *Believe in You . . . Love Being You*

Part Two: *Discover Yourself* and your unique blueprint

Part Three: *You Matter . . . Make Yourself a Priority*

Part Four: *Be Positively Contagious* and share your voice

Part Five: *Ask HOW* to overcome your fears and obstacles

Part Six: *Live Your True Purpose, Brand, and Story of You*

Part Seven: *Bringing It All Together for Your Best Self*

You Rock! Be you — simply be you — the best version of YOU.

Choose the beautiful, unique, and talented you.

You Got This!

Let's Get Started . . .

In a world where you often put other priorities at the top of your list, *Are You Ready?* is an investment and a focus on you. Together, let's connect the dots of your everyday influences to create your best self and live your dream life.

> *"We struggle with the complexities and avoid the simplicities."*
> — Norman Vincent Peale

Simplicity is a gift you give to yourself. A secret to dealing with the *complexities* in your life is by adding *simple* daily actions.

Are You Ready? is a personal take-action journal that helps you navigate your life. You can find your true purpose as you build confidence, become sure of yourself, and discover your best self.

This book is filled with strategies to lift you higher and help you let go of negative self-chatter and self-doubt. Be guided through times when you are insecure or unsure of yourself.

Travel on an inspirational journey and find *why* you love being you. As we journey together and choose you as a priority, you can learn simple techniques on HOW to be a happier, healthier, and re-energized version of YOU.

Imagine . . .
If you were the best version of yourself, how would your future change?
. . . Here is your nudge.

Part One

Believe in You...Love Being You

Part One: Introduction
Believe in You...Love Being You

You'll learn how to:

❖ Appreciate your inner beauty.

❖ Instill an unwavering belief in yourself.

❖ Discover your uniqueness as a gift.

❖ Uncover what you love about yourself.

❖ Choose the message you bring to the world.

❖ Share your voice.

❖ Reflect on a bucket list of adventures.

❖ Imagine your 100-year-old self in a rearview mirror.

❖ Be You. Be authentic and choose your best self.

❖ Learn why to appreciate YOU.

❖ Love being you.

❖ Realize *You Got This!*

Jackie Cantoni

Chapter 1
Believe in You

"Practice believing in you. Choose you."
— Jackie Cantoni

Believe in yourself. Have the courage to believe in yourself. One of my favorite quotes is by Paul Shane Shafer, *"As one person, I cannot change the world, but I can change the world for one person."*

Your goal is to believe, each day, you can be the best version of yourself. Start with yourself and then you can influence those around you—one person at a time.

But how do you believe in yourself? A first step to instilling belief in yourself is to release the perfect-image perception of what your life should look like and embrace you and the life you have. Choose to own and understand who you are today. Then you can discover strategies to appreciate yourself, be grateful for your uniqueness, and love being you!

Can you learn to appreciate your uniqueness from a flower? I love flowers. My husband jokes and says I must have been a bumblebee in a previous life. When I see roses or beautiful wildflowers, I am immersed in their beauty. There is a saying, *"Flowers do not compare themselves to the flower next to them to decide their own beauty."* Flowers do not look outside themselves to see what or how the other flowers are blooming. Why should you?

Today, more than ever, images displayed in the media and the world can make you question your self-worth, especially when you compare yourself to those images. Instead, reflect inwardly and reach deep into your heart to recognize the gifts you bring to the world.

As you go through each day, don't waste your energy by comparing yourself to others. Instead, look inside yourself and identify your own strengths, uniqueness, and talents. Bring value to and focus on your inner beauty. Be authentic. Be you.

Inspirational Self-Affirmations

One strategy to help you boost your self-belief and confidence is to surround yourself daily with positive affirmations, both verbal and written. A verbal affirmation is *optimistic and inspirational self-talk.* It can be on the value you bring each day to yourself, family, career, friends, and life.

Often, you may carry the weight of the world on your shoulders with stress from your daily responsibilities. A self-affirmation can rejuvenate you with new energy and motivation. It can be as simple as looking at yourself in the mirror and sharing *why you appreciate and love YOU.* These are positive attributes and qualities that make you . . . you. Regardless of your social or economic status, positive self-reinforcement can help you overcome or manage daily concerns and build resilience. For example, you can state aloud, "I bring joy to the world with my humor. I am kind. I see the best in others." Think about the inner gifts you bring and remind yourself of them verbally each day. You can also include your internal drive, compassion, willingness to help a friend — whatever is in your heart that defines you.

Even if you are at a low point in your day or life, reach deep within yourself and pull out the positive qualities you bring to the world. Are you a caring person or friend? Are you furthering your education? Are you dedicated at your job? Do you invest in your future to provide financially for yourself or your family? Remind yourself not to let negative influences at work, home, or school penetrate your core and well-being. Challenge yourself to remove any negative self-chatter or self-doubt. Replace this with why you appreciate yourself and the value you bring each day.

"Believe you can and you're halfway there."
— Theodore Roosevelt

To get started, jot down three positive self-affirmations on *why you appreciate you*. These can change daily and are your focus today.

My three self-affirmations for today are:

1. _____

2. _____

3. _____

Next, do you have a favorite written inspirational saying you can place on a sticky note by your bed, on your fridge, or at work? A second strategy is to simply surround yourself with optimistic written affirmations, including motivational quotations or images to uplift your spirit. On my desk is an inspirational sign that states, *"Proceed as if success is inevitable,"* and on our wall is artwork displaying *"Be you."*

Surround yourself with encouraging, uplifting messages to remind you of the uniqueness and joy you bring to the world. Daily positive and inspirational affirmations can become effortless and have a tremendous influence on your attitude and life.

Self-Affirmations — Visualize Your Goals

One more self-affirmation technique is to identify and write down a specific *goal* you want to achieve. Then each day, say your goal aloud and visualize yourself reaching your goal. Take the time to internalize what success will feel and look like to you. This visualization and reinforcement can strengthen your self-belief as you see yourself achieving what is in your heart.

For example:

I am grateful: I will be relaxing 15 minutes a day to re-energize.
I am grateful: I will be playing golf once a week with my friends.
I am grateful: I will be taking x class to further my education.
I am grateful: I will be receiving a promotion into x job at work.
I am grateful: I will be losing 5 pounds by May 21st.

Be as specific as possible and include timeframes to help solidify the objective in your mind. What are three goals for you?

My three goals are:

1. _____

2. _____

3. _____

Practice both your *appreciating you* and *goal self-affirmations* to reinforce your daily self-belief. Build your self-confidence one day at a time.

Remember, a secret to overcoming complexity is introducing simple daily actions. *Self-belief is the cornerstone and foundation to your best self.*

***

I am ready to believe in myself.

***

Actions I'm Choosing for My Best Self

- I will say aloud three positive self-affirmations each day.

- I will display two written inspirational messages.

- I will create a personal goal(s) and visualize success.

Chapter 2
Love Being You

"Don't dim your light because others think it's too bright."
— Jackie Cantoni

This is about YOU . . .

Let's explore and understand YOU. Give yourself permission to focus on yourself for a moment. Oh no, it's self-inventory time. Ugghh!!! Why is thinking about yourself and reflecting on who you might be so difficult? You may often push yourself to the bottom of the list of responsibilities and other priorities filling your days. Do you often sink to the bottom as you take care of others?

It's time to pause. Breathe. And now think about you.

What do you appreciate about yourself? If you had to list 100 traits you love about yourself, could you? Well . . . let's start with 10 and discover your *"Top 10 Traits That I Love about Myself."* Each day continue to add to your list.

Begin with the first item you are most proud of and write it down. This is the first step to identifying each joyful aspect of what makes you . . . YOU!

Are You Ready?

Your *"Top 10 Traits That I Love about Myself"* really is only scratching the surface. At first, it may seem like a stretch out of your comfort zone; however, once you get going, you will love recognizing your gifts. You'll start to realize these traits are only the beginning of who you are on your journey to your best self.

Since creating your *"Top 10 Traits That I Love about Myself"* can be intimidating, here are some thought starters. How about your smile, kindness to help a friend, ability to make others laugh, leadership skills, or your dedication to lifelong learning?

Are you ready to invest in you?

Top 10 Traits That I Love about Myself

1. _____

2. _____

3. _____

4. _____

5. _____

6. _____

7. _____

8. _____

9. _____

10. _____

Doesn't it feel good to reflect on what you love about you? Does the initial feeling of self-guilt begin to drift away as you focus on you and your self-image?

Creating your *"Top 10 Traits That I Love about Myself "*is one of the steppingstones to identifying who you are and what you value in your heart. This reflection will serve as a foundation as you move through the chapters for recognizing your personal brand, true purpose, and belief in yourself.

Remember, *the most important investment you will ever make is in yourself.* Your *"Top 10 Traits That I Love about Myself"* is a place to make you smile when you need a boost in your day.

***

I am ready to love myself.

***

Actions I'm Choosing for My Best Self

- I will identify the *"Top 10 Traits That I Love about Myself."*

- I will reflect each day on what I love about ME.

- I will continue to add to my list recognizing my uniqueness.

Chapter 3
The Best Version of You at Age 100

"And the beauty of a woman, with passing years only grows."
— Audrey Hepburn

Imagine you are 100 years old.

If you could peek into the future and view a resume of your life at age 100, what would you hope to see on it? Whatever your age, take a moment to think 30, 50, 75 or more years into the future. Really. Then ask yourself, what life experiences would you want to see on the resume in front of you? Would you have included your dreams? Would you have realized the passion deep in your heart? Did you *choose being the best version of you* during your life?

You know how quickly life zooms by, and your passions go out of focus. This reflection is a strategy for a happier, more fulfilling life. For your *Best Version of Myself Resume at Age 100* on the next page, jot down the goals or passions sitting in your heart. The ones you want to accomplish before you wake up one day as your 100-year-old self.

The Best Version of Myself Resume at Age 100

Objective: To accomplish these life experiences by age 100. Think of this reflection as your bucket list of adventures and moments you want to enjoy during your life.

A Life Passion(s): _____

Activities I Enjoy: _____

Bucket List Adventures: _____

Volunteer/Stewardship: _____

Work Experiences: _____

Places Traveled: _____

Philanthropy: _____

People Whose Lives I Influenced: _____

Health: _____

Finances: _____

Family: _____

Friendships: _____

Other: _____

Continue to reflect and uncover where you want to be at age 100, then during your *Are You Ready?* journey, you can be guided to fulfill these goals and passions.

***

I am ready to become the best version of myself at age 100.

***

Actions I'm Choosing for My Best Self

- I will jot down my dreams in *The Best Version of Myself Resume at Age 100.*

- I will reflect on my resume as a roadmap to my future.

- I will explore the strategies in *Are You Ready?* to fulfill these goals and passions.

Chapter 4
Share Your Message

"Start with love, then add laughter."
— Jackie Cantoni

As part of a volunteer team, I helped design handmade posters for a young girl who was terminally ill. Her family appreciated the team's support. We all wanted to make a positive difference for her and her family.

As the volunteers came through the door to make their inspirational posters, I watched as they looked at their *blank* poster board. What message could possibly convey the compassion in their hearts for this little girl?

As the morning progressed, the posters came alive. I saw messages of **You Rock!**, **Welcome!**, **Brave!** Each poster was bursting with compassion, positive energy, and kindness. They were ready to bring a smile and joy into the heart of a little girl who had faced a lifetime of struggle. Her courage is what defined her.

You may have heard this question asked about the value of struggle to the human soul, *"If you could put your life into a pile with everyone else's life, and then pick from the pile, which life would you choose to live? Would you pick your own life? Either way, why?"*

Surely, you may wonder if a young girl who was terminally ill and courageously fighting to stay alive may choose someone else's life. It would be unkind and unfair to ask her, or perhaps anyone facing terminal illness, that question. However, in my heart, I believe she is an angel sharing her message with us.

A Future of Opportunities

After volunteering that day, for some reason I stopped and thought about those blank poster boards and the team's messages to the little girl. It was then I realized each day we all start with our own *blank* canvas and share our own *message* with the world.

As you wake up each morning, it's your decision to select the *message you will share with the world*. You decide your message, attitude for the day, and direction you will take your life. Let your uniqueness shine as part of your message. Each day you start with a blank canvas and make these decisions. You decide if you will "go for" the new opportunity or continue doing what you have always done. At times, you may feel your daily choices are made for you by your circumstances, your spouse, children, employer, or parents. The truth is, you control many of these daily decisions, attitudes, actions, and reactions. Your future is a blank canvas waiting to be filled with new opportunities.

As you stare at a future of opportunities, have you ever been overwhelmed, afraid, or too busy to decide how to lead your life?

Change that. Take the first step and realize your life is yours to design. Take a moment and think about an *opportunity* you want to pursue but have feared or thought you were not good enough to attain. It can be a new position at work, an activity at school, or the desire to create a healthier lifestyle.

Jot down the *opportunity* you hold in your heart. Draw on your courage to see the gifts you bring and can share with others each day. Perhaps it's a passion you have wanted to pursue, yet, may have felt stuck and need that next nudge. Then, as we move through the chapters, you will learn the strategies to achieve this goal.

_____

_____

Also, think about your *message* to the world. What message have you wanted to share with others but lacked the courage to act on confidently? If you are stuck and do not know where to start with your message, then "look" at your blank canvas and place a little heart in the upper corner and *start with love.* Then draw a smile in the lower corner and *start with laughter.* Each day let your message to the world begin with *love and laughter.* Then add in what you hold in your heart.

What is your message to the world? Jot down a *message* you want to share with yourself or others today:

_____

_____

Let YOU and your uniqueness be reflected on your canvas each day. Realize, *You Rock!*

***

I am ready to share my message with the world.

***

Actions I'm Choosing for My Best Self

- I will identify an opportunity sitting in my heart.

- I will visualize each day the positive message I want to share with the world.

- I will start my days with love and laughter.

Chapter 5
Your Voice

"A lot of people are afraid to say what they want,
that's why they don't get what they want."
— Madonna

We all have our personal challenges; some days they are bigger than others. Regardless of their size, they are *our* struggles, and we must develop the resilience and tools to overcome them. Once conquered, the obstacles quite often define us, and inspire others.

Whether it is a family crisis, personal struggle, or not being able to open the lid on a jelly jar, in the moment of strife your approach to how you handle the situation can make all the difference.

My journey, on one challenging day, began with excitement and ended with weary red eyes. It was a simple decision, so I thought. I wanted to have the entire interior of our home painted. The painters had a cancellation and now would be arriving in just two days. Excited about our new project, I drove to the local design gallery to select the paint colors. Then, time stood still as I stared at piles of swatches and stacks of books full of options. It was overwhelming. How can there be 100 shades of yellow? I was unable to grasp this many paint colors knowing they would be on our walls for years to come. The negative self-chatter began to fill my mind. I thought, *"Why can't I pick a color to paint a wall!?"* I left the design gallery and arrived home with weary red eyes.

Have you ever been self-conscious or discouraged because you do not have the same skillset or talent as a co-worker or friend? As a lesson learned, embrace the areas you are still developing and do not hide them. Be you. Accept and own who you are today. Choose to learn about it or decide it's not your focus or priority.

For me, my husband, who saw my weary eyes and listened to my story, called a friend who was experienced with colors and hues. He helped us blend the paint shades from room to room. The result? Room colors we loved!

Is choosing paint colors a true challenge? For me it was. Let's not judge another's journey. The lesson I want to share is to *realize and embrace the power of your voice.*

Three Powerful Ways to Use Your Voice

1 Ask for Help.

You don't always have to be a superhero. You may believe you have superhero powers; however, at times even superheroes need the help of others too. Ask. Ask. Ask . . . Ask for help.

As you reflect on your best self, ask someone who can see your vision and help you bring your dreams to life. This is the same if you need assistance with a project at work, school, or daily responsibilities at home — *plan to use your voice to ask others for their support.* You may often hold onto your struggles or challenges as they fester inside of you. Let today be the last day a concern gnaws at you.

Can you become comfortable reaching out and asking for guidance and help from mentors, family members, co-workers, and friends? Life is meant to be lived in teams. When you ask for support or assistance, you can succeed as part of a team. Release the need to do it alone and be a superhero. You have a community around you — ask for support on your journey.

For example, think about your *"Best Version of Myself Resume at Age 100"* and whether there is someone who can assist you to achieve one of your goals. Do you need support with a project at home, an assignment at school, or career advice at work but have been afraid to ask? Are you looking to start a new business as an entrepreneur or choosing the next steps for your education and could benefit from a mentor? What do you need help with?

This is your nudge. *Be intentional. Take action.* At times, to let your light shine, you may need guidance from others. Think about how someone else's assistance can be beneficial to you.

I will ask for guidance or assistance with:

_____

_____

2 Share Your Voice to Help Others.

Second, let your voice be heard to display the talents and gifts you bring to the world. Your uniqueness is a gift. Share you.

When you are in a social setting, work meeting, or classroom and someone asks for feedback or input, *instead of being quiet, think of and share something meaningful and relevant that adds to the conversation.* For example, what is one of your strengths that will help others to overcome challenges? Be prepared to share your opinions after reflecting on what would be of value. Remember, *You Rock!* Believe in yourself with confidence as you share your uniqueness and value.

One way I share my voice is through mentoring. I vividly recall being introduced to one of my new mentees. After we shook hands and started talking, I noticed he did not make eye contact with me. At first, I felt a sense of disrespect; however, as we began to build our relationship, I soon realized he had a lack of self-confidence. This young man with lots of hidden potential did not appear to have a strong external support system or an optimistic belief in himself — not yet, anyway!

During our conversations, I focused on encouragement and positive feedback on his projects. My purpose was to inspire him to believe in himself. As time passed, my mentee began to clearly see his value. He now saw the many talents he brings to the world.

How can you and your voice have a positive influence on others?

For me, I may not be great at selecting paint colors; however, I appreciate my ability and share my voice to mentor others.

As a self-challenge, pick one area in your life where you can help someone with your uniqueness and talents.

I will share my voice during/doing:

_____

_____

A final note on sharing your voice: interestingly, being heard, at times, can also be *remaining silent or listening*. Listening is a powerful way to share your voice as a support to a mentee or friend.

3 Internalize Your Voice for Self-Belief.

The third way to use your voice is through your daily verbal affirmations, which we explored in Chapter One. Continue to use your voice with encouraging words for a positive self-belief.

***

I am ready to share my voice.

***

Actions I'm Choosing for My Best Self

- I will use my voice to ask for support with a project at home, school, or work.

- I will share my voice and talents to help others.

- I will *listen* to a friend who needs a comforting shoulder.

Chapter 6
It's Your Choice

"Try your best or choose your best. It's your choice."
— Jackie Cantoni

Try your best. How many times have you heard someone say, *try your best*? Are you ready to change your mindset to *choose* your best?

You can *choose to be your best* each day — even during the activities you may or may not enjoy. You can choose to be your best-self while spending time with family and friends. You can choose to do your best when completing your job responsibilities. You can choose how to best react to a disappointment. You can choose to make better decisions on healthier choices. You can choose moments of solitude to replenish your soul. Each day you choose your attitude. You choose your actions and reactions. Why not *choose* your best?

Do you have recurring patterns in your life? Whether you create happy inner feelings or feel sorry for yourself, or whether you are the hero in your own life story or the victim, it's your choice. Do you know others, or have you ever experienced a "whiner" moment, full of complaints? Although sometimes life seems to happen to you, it's essential to recognize you *make* many of the choices in your day. Respectfully, it's time to take ownership and accountability for your life. Each day you choose. Own your choices.

Stop and think of the hundreds of choices you make each week and the influence they have on your attitude and your life. Often you are making choices and may not even be aware of it. Right now, you are choosing to become the best version of yourself.

You choose what time you go to bed at night, which affects your energy level the next day. You choose if your morning starts with relaxation or rushing. When you arrive home from work, do you plop on the couch or spend time on one of your priorities? Remember this is about YOU . . . *choosing you.*

Have you ever been disappointed with a choice in the past? For thought starters, were you upset because your child did not clean up after herself? Were you stressed because you were late to work or school? Or unhappy your favorite pants were getting too tight?

Disappointment may often stem from the choices we make. Take a moment to reflect on the past week and the moments when you felt disappointment with yourself or someone else and jot them down here:

1. _____

2. _____

How can your new choices change your outcomes listed above?

    1. _____

    2. _____

You choose whether you will use your voice and clearly communicate expectations with your child for a clean room. You choose to wake up a little earlier to be early for work or school. You choose to fit into your pants when you decide to eat the veggies versus the cupcakes at the party. You choose to say positive self-affirmations to nourish your soul.

The best or most appropriate choices are not always easy.

One technique to guide your actions is to increase your awareness of each choice. Stop and think of the choices you will have to make. Plan ahead for bigger choices upcoming that day, week, month, or year. Your approach to how you make a choice is a habit and a life skill. It's an essential strategy to happier days.

As you reflect on YOU, remember, you hold the key with the power of your choice. You will no longer only *try* your best— you will now *choose* your personal best.

Choose to be the best version of YOU!

***

I am ready to choose to be my personal best.

***

Actions I'm Choosing for My Best Self

- I will reflect on the past week and realize the *power* of my choices.

- I will be mindful of how choice is a strategy and life skill.

- I will realize how my choices can influence disappointment or joy in my life.

- I will *choose* to be the best version of myself.

Chapter 7
What is Your Sentence for Today?

"The only people who don't tumble
are those who never mount the high wire."
— Oprah Winfrey

As you now know, your daily attitude and happiness can be your choice.

Tonight, when you go to bed, grab a piece of paper and a pen, and place them by your bed. First thing in the morning when you wake up, write three *"Today I choose to"* sentences.

Let your three *"Today I choose to"* action statements inspire you on your journey to your best self. To start, set small daily goals like:

1. *Today I choose to* walk on the treadmill for 30 minutes.
2. *Today I choose to* study an extra hour on my homework.
3. *Today I choose to* contact three sales prospects.
4. *Today I choose to* put down my cellphone and give a loved one a heartfelt hug.

Now let's begin to think about you. Below, fill in what you want to accomplish today. These bite-size actions are only for today.

1 My three *"Today I choose to"* actions are:

1. *Today I choose to* _____

2. *Today I choose to* _____

3. *Today I choose to* _____

Nice job focusing on yourself. Feel good about what you wrote. Do not judge them or you. Just feel good you have three *"Today I choose to"* actions for the day. These can kick-start you and each daily action will add up. To show the power of your manageable bite-size daily actions, if you contact three prospects a day for 30 days, then you will have contacted 90 prospects. Each small accomplishment adds up on your journey to achieving your goal.

2 Expand Your Thinking . . . Create Momentum

As you get into the routine of your *"Today I choose to"* actions, then you can challenge yourself to expand your thinking and **create an action for other areas in your life.** For example: what would you choose to do at *work*? Is there something new you could do at *home* or that pertains to your *health*? What is meaningful for you?

Jot down some thoughts here:

Self and Health:

Today I choose to: _____

Relationships:

Today I choose to: _____

Work or School:

Today I choose to: _____

Life — My Future:

Today I choose to: _____

The key to your *"Today I choose to"* actions is they are only for *today.* Then you can accomplish each action, each day. Besides feeling good, these provide a daily focus. Move forward one action item at a time.

***

I am ready and inspired to accomplish my simple daily actions.

***

Actions I'm Choosing for My Best Self

- I will write my three *Today I choose to* daily actions.

- I will focus on today, accomplishing my goals one day at a time.

- I will create daily actions to positively influence my health, my work, my relationships, and my future. I own this!

Chapter 8
You Got This!

"When something is important enough,
you do it even if the odds are not in your favor."
— Elon Musk

You've Got This! or for the purpose of this book the more commonly stated version is *You Got This!*

As you journey through your day, look internally and continue to build your self-confidence. The answers are often right inside you, but you know to courageously ask others if you need their help. First, look within. And always remember, *You Got This!*

As a young adult, I attended a large conference where the guest speaker was president of a Fortune 50 company. After the presentation, I wanted to introduce myself. I recall the self-doubt filling my mind as I thought about speaking with him. Why was I so nervous to say hello to a guest speaker? My thoughts were filled with negative self-chatter as to *why* he would *not* want to talk with *me*. My mind was formulating a negative outcome before anything even happened! How often do you sabotage yourself and not even give yourself a chance because of self-doubt?

Are You Ready?

After the president's speech to the large crowd, I paused and began to practice positive self-affirmations including *I Got This!* In my mind I was repeatedly saying, *I Got This!* as I took the first step. I did not have any space in my thoughts for self-doubt. This positive self-affirmation wiped away the negative chatter and replaced my fear, encouraging me to approach him. Before I knew it, I was standing in front of him. I introduced myself and spoke about the significance of his presentation and the influence it had on me.

He was very gracious and welcoming. Interestingly, the original outcome that played in my mind did not materialize. I was grateful to believe in myself to take a small risk.

We often regret what we do not do, more than what we do.

As Lewis Carroll inspires us:

> *"In the end . . . we only regret the chances we didn't take,*
> *the relationships we were afraid to have,*
> *and the decisions we waited too long to make."*

I find when I whisper *I Got This!* to myself, a smile comes across my face and I straighten my shoulders. Just saying *I Got This!* gives me a boost of courage and faith in myself to move forward.

In life, you must reach deep into your heart and pull out the tiny seed of self-belief. For some, the seed has been fertilized with encouragement and has grown over time, while some people have their seed of self-belief sitting dormant or had it stomped on by others and now need it to be nurtured with self-love.

I Got This! I Got This! Doesn't it feel good saying it to yourself? *I Got This!* is a simple self-affirmation you can mindfully repeat to build your confidence and give yourself that nudge to meet someone new, present to an audience, interview for a job, or face a new challenge.

Remember, when you hear negative self-chatter, just choose to replace it and say *I Got This!*

***

I am ready to say, "I Got This!"

***

Actions I'm Choosing for My Best Self

- I will say *I Got This!* for new opportunities.

- I will remember to replace negative self-chatter and self-doubt with *I Got This!*

Part One Take-Aways
Believe in You...Love Being You

Simple treasures to nudge you on your journey to becoming the best version of yourself.

- Believe in yourself.

- Celebrate your uniqueness.

- Focus internally on your gifts and talents.

- Start your day with positive self-affirmations.

- Discover your *"Top 10 Traits That I Love about Myself."*

- Create *"The Best Version of Myself Resume at Age 100."*

- Share your voice.

- *Choose* your message to the world each day.

- Focus on your *Today I Choose to* simple daily actions.

- Remember *You Rock!*

- Start your days with love and laughter.

- Choose to be your personal best.

- Remind yourself *I Got This!*

Part Two

Discovering You

Part Two: Introduction
Discovering You

You'll learn how to:

- ❖ Reflect on how much time you spend planning your life to become your best self.

- ❖ Discover increased happiness, energy, and joy.

- ❖ Enjoy your experiences from a place of gratitude instead of entitlement.

- ❖ Bring back some of your youthful energy and childhood belief in yourself.

- ❖ Appreciate what you do have in this moment.

- ❖ Give yourself the gift of caring, supporting people in your life.

- ❖ Take the time to make your relationships intentional.

- ❖ Disconnect to reconnect.

- ❖ Stay in your lane.

- ❖ Make the world a kinder place by spreading a little kindness.

Jackie Cantoni

Chapter 9
Find Your Inner Child

"Once in a while someone amazing comes along . . . and here I am."
— Tigger, A.A. Milne

Think of your childhood. Can you bring back some of your youthful energy and carefree spirit? As you move through life, responsibilities may fill your days, along with pressure and worry. Reflect and draw upon the attributes of your childhood. Think about some of your lighthearted traits and take moments to be curious.

Let the weight of the world be released and live in the moment. Lie in the grass. Walk barefoot. Sit and watch the clouds go by. Walk in the rain. Be playful. Let your inner child guide you. As a child, if someone asked you, "What do you want to be when you grow up?", you always had an answer. There were no limitations. Today, let's begin with that same mindset.

Do you put limits on yourself? Realize your age has no limit and is truly only a number. If you want to go back to school and you are 63, then go back to school. If you want to start your own business or paint a masterpiece for the art gallery and you are 22 or 52, then invest in yourself and plan step by step how to accomplish what is in your heart.

Creativity and imagination are your building blocks as you become the best version of yourself. Unfortunately, people at times lose creativity and imagination as they age. Often, as we enter adulthood our passions can get derailed. Do you *put off* your dreams because you think they cannot be materialized?

I mentioned my love of flowers and how my husband jokes I was a bumblebee in a previous life. Passions and dreams are like flowers since they both begin to grow with a seed. Your imagination is a seed that can create endless opportunities. All you have to do is think like a bumblebee:

"Aerodynamically, the bumblebee shouldn't be able to fly, but the bumblebee doesn't know it, so it goes on flying anyway."
— Mary Kay Ash

When developing an idea or setting a goal, you plant a seed. As time passes, you either nurture the idea with positive thoughts or you smother the idea with negative self-doubt, not allowing it to grow. From now on, let your ideas grow using your imagination and belief — deep within you — from childhood. Do this for you. Reach deep within and find a way to let your seed take root and sprout. Then, with each step, watch your idea grow.

Children believe in themselves before the world starts to tell them otherwise. *How many times does a child fall and get back up? How often do you hear a parent of a young child say, "She has a mind of her own?"* Recapture that childhood belief, remembering what you love deep down and what is important to you. *Have a mind of your own* and accomplish what sits in your heart.

The Smiley

You most likely noticed the smiley face at the beginning of each chapter. This is the smiley I would draw to dot the "i" in my name when I was a young girl. I carried it into adulthood and still enjoy sending handwritten cards with my smiley as part of my note. Stay true to yourself. You have it in you. *Be you* and *share you* with the world.

***

I am ready to bring back my youthful energy.

***

Actions I'm Choosing for My Best Self

- I will pick one activity and approach it with youthful energy.

- I will draw upon the belief from my childhood heart where opportunities are endless, and dreams can be materialized.

Chapter 10
So What? . . . Life is Perspective

*"When you look back on your life,
what will truly matter to you?"*
— Jackie Cantoni

It's a boy! You can probably imagine the joy as a mom and dad to welcome a beautiful baby boy into our lives.

I want to share a little about my family and my *"So What? . . . Life is Perspective"* lesson I learned.

This joyous moment was preceded by a high-risk, bed-ridden pregnancy. The doctor's order was I remain on a mattress for three months since this rest would help the baby grow. My parents, in-laws, and sister, Diane, visited to assist in caring for me and our two-year-old active son, James.

The doctors were concerned the baby was at risk. They asked if we wanted to perform amniocentesis since the baby was small in utero, with little amniotic fluid indicating he may have Down syndrome. Our answer was no. This was our little boy, and he would be a part our lives regardless of his diagnosis. There was no benefit in performing an intrusive test on him or me.

After three months of steroid shots that puffed my cheeks, making me look like a chipmunk, and lying on a mattress, bedridden, it was time to deliver our baby. As the doctor said, "It's a boy," our hearts were filled with joy. We named our second son Nathaniel (Nathan) Joshua, which means a gift from God. My mother-in-law, Rosalie, suggested his name and we knew in our hearts it was meant for him. Nathan truly was our second precious gift from God.

He began the first few weeks of his young life in the Neonatal Intensive Care Unit. His little body was connected to wires and tubes helping him grow. Soon the day came when he was strong enough to come home with us.

Within the first few months at home, his tiny hands started to repetitively shake back and forth. It was a rhythmic motion, starting then stopping, repeating over and over. As a new mom, I did not recognize this movement and called our high-risk pregnancy specialist. I recall how quickly she was to identify the activity as a seizure. At three months old, Nathan was diagnosed with epilepsy, a seizure disorder. I had heard of this but was not quite sure what it really meant for our baby or us.

I remember worrying about how he would be able to drive on his 16th birthday if he had a seizure diagnosis. I was worrying 16 years into the future with no idea of what the next 16 months would hold for our family. Looking back, this worrying added nothing except anxiety to my family or our lives.

Are You Ready?

Three more months passed, and Nathan was not developing physically as a typical baby. It was recommended we take him to a neurologist. At six months old, he was diagnosed with cerebral palsy.

As little as I knew about seizures, I knew even less about cerebral palsy (CP). I started to research and had stacks of medical reports and analyses. What is CP and what does it mean for our son's life? Will he be able to walk? He wasn't rolling or, never mind, even crawling as you expect babies to do.

Three more months passed, and we were advised to take him to an ophthalmologist. *Our heads were already spinning with the diagnoses of epilepsy and cerebral palsy; now at nine months old, our son was diagnosed with cortical visual impairment and was legally blind.*

Nathan had not even reached his first birthday. I cried. What kind of life would he lead with all these diagnoses?

Well, something happened after his first birthday. Through the grace of God, Nathan gave us the strength to move past the diagnoses and see him as a beautiful little boy who would be bringing so much joy and love into our hearts and home.

He was not able to walk, talk, or see; however, he understood and knew love. He was kind and gentle and put our lives into a new perspective.

We became grateful almost daily for some of the simple things in life that previously we felt entitled to, including being able to see, walk, and talk. It also enlightened me as to how many times we often take our lives and everyday abilities for granted.

Our son may never "see a sunset" or say, "I love you, Mommy." Life is truly put into perspective when you witness every day someone who has different abilities or challenges. More than twenty years later, Nathan is quadriplegic in a wheelchair and remains unable to talk or see; however, he continues to exude so much joy and love. Each day is different and there is so much unknown. In my heart, I believe God gave Nathan to us for a reason. His giggles are contagious, and he is one of the happiest, most beautiful people I know.

We continue to not know what the future holds, but we take one day at a time — living inch by inch because none of us knows what tomorrow will bring. That is why we are to be grateful and appreciative of today. Perspective is in the eye of the beholder and truly is a choice based upon your acceptance and reaction to circumstances.

Shift in Perspective
Determine what is truly important to you. Then, as you encounter issues at work, home, or school that do not directly impact one of your critical priorities, it may be easier to put those concerns into perspective. For me, core priorities are my faith, family, friends, health, and safety.

Day to day, do you often waste energy and wear yourself down over activities to which you should be saying *"So what?"* instead of reacting? Sometimes there are circumstances in life that may upset you, yet when you reflect on whether they are truly priorities, you can ask yourself, "Is it worth my energy?"

Reflect on your past week. Were there times when you became frustrated or irritated with a co-worker, family member, schoolmate, or even yourself? Did you lose patience with a customer service representative who was trying to assist you? Negatively reacting and internalizing this type of frustration can deplete your energy. Sometimes, it's helpful to put these situations into perspective and ask yourself, "Is this one of my critical priorities?" If not, then maybe you can choose a different response.

An Inconvenience

As continuous interactions are part of your day-to-day life, you want to distinguish between an *inconvenience* and a critical concern. Many of your daily frustrations may truly only be annoyances. The traffic is backed up, there is a line at the grocery store, soccer practice is running behind schedule, or perhaps the file at work is just taking a long time to open.

Although many times these can be frustrating or inconvenient, can you have a new perspective and ask yourself whether the situation is life-threatening? Also, probe further with, "Can I change these circumstances?" For example, does the traffic get backed up at the same time each day on your way to work or school? Can you choose to leave earlier, take an alternative route, or be more accepting of the results? How about being grateful for the quiet time in your car? Or even better, appreciate you have a car that can get stuck in traffic! It's surprising how your thoughts can affect your mood.

What if you are scheduled to receive a package, and it gets rescheduled for a later delivery. Ask yourself, did it contain lifesaving supplies or was it merely a pair of the latest celebrity sneakers? Of course, you can be disappointed if you were excited to get your package, but by keeping your perspective, you can enjoy your days and experiences from a place of gratitude instead of entitlement.

This quote by Henry David Thoreau is one of my all-time favorite sayings.

"It's not what you look at that matters, it is what you see."

One secret to life is to have a positive and optimistic perspective each day. This one hidden treasure can have a tremendous influence on your life. How you view and react to your daily circumstances can inspire your mood, energy, and well-being. An uplifting perspective is a key to happiness.

***

I am ready to be grateful for the moment.

***

Actions I'm Choosing for My Best Self

- I will ask myself *"So what?"* when an experience is really only an *inconvenience*. Then I will choose my attitude.

- I will pick one situation that repeatedly seems to be an inconvenience and choose to change the outcome.

Chapter 11
Stay in Your Lane

"I'm not in competition with anyone but myself.
My goal is to beat my last performance."
— Celine Dion

How often do you view others' lives and lose focus on your own? Can you release looking at the competition and focus on you?

When writing this book, I had this "aha!" moment. I realized I didn't focus on my competition growing up. My attitude in school, relationships, work, and sports was focused on the experience. It was not on beating or competing with the other person. I was simply focused on being *the best version of me.*

I want to be humble as I say what's next, so please forgive me if it comes across braggadocious. By focusing on being *the best version of me,* in high school I received the Most Hustle Award in basketball, the Most Congeniality Award in cheerleading, the Ms. Home Economics Award, and the Best Smile Award.

Again, I say these not as a brag, but as a lesson. I was never specifically trying to achieve any of these. I was being me and not trying to compare myself or compete with others. This I owe to my parents and sister who made me, *the chubby cheeks girl with braces, feel like a confident and beautiful swan.*

If at work, school, or when viewing online images, you focus on the competition — the other classmate, friends, or co-worker — you can lose your focus and internal drive. Your energy is spent on worrying about someone else. It is wasted energy, taking your eye off what you can do to improve yourself. When viewing your peers or acquaintances, *stay in your lane*. Yes, stay in your lane and focus your energy on YOU.

Do you often compare yourself to others? It's okay to be mindful of those around you. However, eliminate the anxiety associated with the comparison; let go of trying to compete for attention or trying to be someone you are not so that you can "fit in."

If "friends" are going out and you are not invited, instead of focusing on your disappointment, refocus your energy on a priority or activity you enjoy. Consider calling a friend with whom you haven't talk with in a while and nurture that relationship. Or take the time to enjoy a relaxing activity to replenish and rejuvenate you. *Choose* to focus on you and your priorities.

Keep Your Eye on Your Dreams

Imagine if you had the dream of writing a cookbook. Creating a recipe masterpiece of foods with color, flavor, and nutritional value that will make the reader's mouth water thinking about your tasty options. Yum! Then, one day, you walk into a bookstore and see more than 50 cookbooks on the shelf. Oh, No!

Now, the way you respond to this competition and internalize it can determine your future drive and motivation. It can be discouraging to see those chefs smiling back at you from the front of their cookbooks. Your face should be there alongside theirs. If you compare yourself and internalize it, your pace may slow because of the competition.

However, if your focus is on you and your love of cooking, then you can remember the talent you have and why you thought of writing a cookbook in the first place.

When you find yourself spending too much time on your competition, take the first step to recognize this as a habit you can change. Then shift your thinking to re-focus on one of your priorities. As with many habits, you can choose to change this behavior one day at a time.

Since anxiety from comparison is so prominent, let's look at one additional technique. Try this . . . when you find yourself competitively thinking about a peer, co-worker, or online image, say to yourself, *"I choose to refocus and invest my energy in me."* Then take the first action step to take care of you.

Let's be intentional. Reflect and place an image in your mind of someone you frequently compare yourself to. Then remind yourself by stating, *"I will no longer compare myself to (state their name.) I will release the competitive vibe and shift my energy to focus on me and to better myself."*

It's not always easy with the stimuli of social media and the news showing you your competition. It can be deflating and discouraging at times. You must *make the choice* not to let the external or competition penetrate your soul. Instead, concentrate on you and remember the strategy to *Stay in Your Lane.*

It's simply a nudge to *consider replacing competitive energy with a picture of success for yourself.*

***

I am ready to stay in my lane.

***

Actions I'm Choosing for My Best Self

- I will release the competitive vibe, especially when viewing other's online images.

- I will state aloud that I am going to shift my energy and focus on one of my priorities.

- I will stay in my lane, remember my uniqueness, and believe in ME.

Chapter 12
Connections and Friendships

"The best thing to hold onto in life is each other."
— Audrey Hepburn

Have you ever walked through a retail store and noticed people who looked detached, distant, or unconnected? You see it every day. This is especially true during the holidays. At times, people are overscheduled or exhausted and they lose their relaxed, friendly connection with others. What has happened to humanity? Why have we become so detached from each other?

Like a puppy dog that greets you with a wagging tail, my husband is beyond friendly. He wears his heart on his sleeve. He will start a conversation or talk to just about anyone. However, I notice initially some people can be hesitant about his kindness and sincerity since this neighborly connection is becoming a lost trait. I think in years past, people relied on each other more than they do today. Historically, there seemed to be more community and connectedness.

Let's seek to open our hearts and bring a small piece of that community contact back.

Disconnect to Reconnect

As you think about reconnecting with others, can you begin to disconnect from your devices, computers, and phones to look up and see each other? Today, with technology at your fingertips, you must choose to *disconnect to reconnect*.

Connections are a secret survival strategy. You may take for granted your relationships and the influence they have on your life and well-being. When relationships are truly a priority in your life, allow yourself to show their importance over routine chores or even the latest news story streaming across your smartphone.

How often do you look down at your cellphone while someone is talking to you? From my experience, it's a form of addiction. However, so many of us do it that it appears to be the norm. The bonding with others can be missing. The use of technology has become a deterrent to giving your attention to something more valuable — another person.

You can often get wrapped up in viewing the online lives of others through social media. It's fun to connect online. However, in large batches, whether you realize it or not, these viewings can subconsciously derail you. You can begin to think, *"How come they can do this, and I can't?"* *These online images can appear to depict someone else's perfect life.* The act of sharing and connecting with others is one thing, but the continuous obsession of viewing another's life may not always be in your best interest. It can distract you from building true relationships.

Connections Are a Gift to Yourself

*"You can't stay in the corner of your forest
waiting for others to come to you.
You have to go to them sometimes."*
— Winnie the Pooh, A.A. Milne

Each Sunday for more than 10 years, I called my mom, who lived in a different state, to do the Jumble Word Scramble puzzle in the Sunday paper. It was our time to connect. My dad was in the background on speaker phone with his entertaining jokes. His stories were so funny, I would belly laugh aloud with tears running down my checks. I treasured this planned time together.

When our "special times" are scheduled, it gives us something to look forward to in our week. Planning for lunch with a friend or a golf date can make the days pass with eager anticipation. Relationships and connections need to be cultivated like a garden. If you neglect them, they can dry up and wither away.

Relationships must be intentional.

I always admired how my mom would call her sister, Mary, who lived thousands of miles away, every Thursday at 1 p.m. This ritual continued until Auntie Mary passed away at 98 years old.

Can you plan to place an important relationship at the top of your priority list? How about adding their name to your *Me List*? It's a gift to yourself to have strong, caring, supportive people in your life. Challenge yourself to reach out to a friend and schedule a phone call to chat or a lunch date. Life passes quickly, and often these connections need to be planned and intentional to stay in touch.

Personally, I remember when my son James was little, I would squat down on my knees, look into his eyes, be patient, and listen with enthusiasm to his entire story, knowing in my heart it was one of the most important stories I would be hearing that day.

How can you nurture one of your relationships?

Choose one relationship within your family, friends, work, or school to focus on this week. Jot down your intention below.

I choose to make (insert name) _____ *a priority.*

I will schedule (an activity) _____ *with him or her.*

Intimate Relationships — Celebrate Each Other

When dating, it's best to be yourself. You want to be with someone who loves you for who you are. If you are sincere, then you can attract someone who loves the authentic you. Relationships and connections should be built on trust and integrity. Appreciate and value yourself, then you can meet a partner who sees that in you.

If you are in a healthy marriage, then remember each day why you fell in love with your spouse. Let him or her be themselves. It's not always effortless to do this, especially with over-scheduled lives. Choose to keep your spouse and your relationship as a priority. Be each other's advocate and biggest fan. Hold hands more often or affectionately touch each other as you walk by each other at home. Connect. Schedule and block off time on the calendar to be together. Plan a date night even if it is time at home. Laugh together. Smile and stare into each other's eyes when you talk. Place a love note on the bathroom mirror or under a pillow.

"Don't chase people. Be yourself, do your own thing, and work hard.
The right people — the ones who really belong in your life —
will come to you. And stay."
—Will Smith

People need to be there for each other for support, love, or even when crises arise. Friendships and relationships are an essential part of your days. It's not the volume of friends as much as it is the deep connections with those who are valued. Treasure and nurture each one. To have caring, supporting people in your life is a priceless gift.

A Relationship with Yourself

Do you love yourself? It sounds simple, yet if I asked you, "what or whom do you love?" would you mention yourself? Begin to be grateful for you and your uniqueness. Lift yourself up with encouragement. Appreciate the times you may have a quirky behavior. Celebrate being you. Remember to nurture, love, and respect yourself. This is a simple reminder to love being you.

***

I am ready to reconnect with myself and others.

***

Actions I'm Choosing for My Best Self

- I will disconnect from my devices, look up, actively listen, and be present with others.

- I will pick one activity to reconnect with a friend.

- I will choose one person and tell him or her why I love them.

Chapter 13
Let's Make a Day of It

"Spread love everywhere you go.
Let no one ever come to you without leaving happier."
—Mother Teresa

Live your life from a place of kindness. It is often the missed opportunities to show kindness you may regret when you look back on your life. Sometimes it is the kind word or just a smile to brighten someone else's day. Or even being kind to yourself.

Challenge yourself to have a day of kindness. *Pick a day. Keep it to yourself.* For each person you encounter, plan to go out of your way to be kind. Begin with a compliment, smile, hug, or a kind act. Think about one person who often frustrates you and approach your conversation from a place of kindness. At the end of the day, reflect on how you felt about your interactions. It's remarkable how doing good for others can lead to a greater sense of purpose and energy in your life. It can be re-energizing for you. When you give kindness to others, think of it as sprinkling perfume on a friend and having some of the scent land on you.

Could one meaning or purpose, within your life, be as simple as making the world a kinder place by spreading a little kindness?

Pass it on . . .

Are You Ready?

***

I am ready to spread kindness.

***

Actions I'm Choosing for My Best Self

- I will pick a day, without anyone else knowing, and be kind with each interaction.

- I will pick one person who often frustrates me and approach our conversation from a place of kindness.

- I will be kind to myself.

Part Two Take-Aways
Discovering You
*Simple treasures to nudge you on your journey
to becoming the best version of yourself.*

- Bring back your youthful spirit.

- Stay in your lane.

- Replace competitive energy with a picture of success for yourself.

- Share your *best self* every day with the world.

- Disconnect to reconnect.

- Appreciate and nurture relationships.

- Remember why you fell in love with your spouse.

- Release the weight of the world and live in the moment.

- Walk barefoot. Lie in the grass. Watch the clouds go by.

- Ask yourself, "So what?" for an inconvenience.

- Share a kind word or smile to brighten someone's day.

- Stay true to yourself. *Be you* and *share you* with the world.

Are You Ready?

Part Three

You Matter . . .
Make Yourself a Priority

Part Three: Introduction
You Matter . . . Make Yourself a Priority

You'll learn how to:

❖ Say Yes to YOU!

❖ Become a top priority in your life.

❖ Release "I'm so busy" and focus on what brings you joy.

❖ Choose to be the healthiest version of you. It is a choice.

❖ Embrace a *Me List* full of your passions and interests.

❖ Follow your heart as you discover your dreams.

❖ Do the *nothing of your choice.*

❖ Release your guilt and rejuvenate you.

❖ Plan financially to realize your goal.

❖ Have *"peace, happiness, and healthiness"* in your life.

❖ Replenish your energy and take care of you.

Jackie Cantoni

Chapter 14
7 Days of You . . . A *Me List*

"The only way to do great work is to love what you do.
If you haven't found it yet, keep looking; don't settle."
— Steve Jobs

Do you have a *Me List*? What is a *Me List*? A *Me List* can include passions, activities, and interests to help you find and take care of YOU!

Think about your life. Is it jam-packed with activities that overwhelm your day, including work assignments, children's activities, schoolwork, or household responsibilities? You may also have a grocery list on your phone or even a sticky note attached to your dashboard with a list of errands.

You plan time for work and your family; however, do you plan a list of enjoyable moments just for you? Can you schedule *"Me Time"* for you, time to nourish and replenish you and your energy?

In the notes section of your smartphone or at the top of a piece of paper, jot down the words *Me List*. Then, as you journey through your days write down, one by one, activities or priorities to take care of YOU.

1 **To get you started, here is an example of a *Me List*.**

Me List Example
Take a 20-minute walk after dinner.

2 **Now it is your turn to jot down one taking care of you item.**

Me List

_____

3 **Next expand your *Me List* and add a daily item for 7 Days.**

For each of the seven days, think of one 10- to 20-minute activity centered on you. You can focus on your health, passion, interests, or whatever else brings you joy. This is time to rejuvenate and energize YOU.

Here is an example:

7 Days of YOU . . . A Me List Example

Day 1: Find my old paint set and paintbrush.
Day 2: Buy a new paint canvas and an art book on techniques.
Day 3: Sketch an outline on my canvas and begin painting.
Day 4: Take a 15-minute nap or relax to re-energize.
Day 5: Paint on my canvas for 15 minutes.
Day 6: Do yoga or take a 20-minute walk with a friend.
Day 7: Paint on my canvas for 15 minutes.

Are You Ready?

This example focuses on an individual who has a love of painting and wants to reintroduce this passion into her life. She also wants to plan some relaxation time to re-energize herself.

What is sitting in your heart? Can you plan time for yourself? Below, jot down a *10- to 20-minute "taking care of you" activity* on each day, as a gift to yourself.

7 Days of YOU . . . A *Me List*

Day 1: _____

Day 2: _____

Day 3: _____

Day 4: _____

Day 5: _____

Day 6: _____

Day 7: _____

Once you see and feel the results after 7 days, then stretch yourself to writing *30 Days of YOU*, with one or more "taking care of you" interests on each day for a month. You can create your *Me List* on your calendar, smartphone, or a piece of paper. Plan these daily priorities to rejuvenate and re-energize YOU.

***

I am ready to have a Me List and become a priority in my life.

***

Actions I'm Choosing for My Best Self

- I will create a *Me List.*

- I will plan 10 to 20 minutes a day to rejuvenate and re-energize me.

- I will schedule my *Me List* activities on my calendar.

Chapter 15
Say YES to You

"The difference between successful people and really successful people is that really successful people say no to almost everything."
— Warren Buffet

Can you learn to say "no?" Saying no to something you don't want to do means saying yes to something more important in your life. Choose to say "yes" to you.

At times, especially for women and young girls, there is a guilt that comes with saying no to others' needs. You may be asked to volunteer at work, school, or a child's activity when you are already overscheduled. Yet, by even politely saying "no" to the request, you may feel as if you will disappoint the person asking.

How about you? Are you letting yourself down if you are exhausted and cannot take care of yourself?

Saying no does not mean you care, love, or respect others less. There is a difference between compassion and helping a friend, family, or co-worker versus not agreeing to be on one more sub-committee that does not interest you. A kind response when asked can be, "Thank you for thinking of me; however, I am unable to volunteer at this time and will let someone else have this opportunity." It's okay to say no.

When my son James was in elementary school, he asked me, "Mom, why don't you become a 'room mom' for my class?" I said, with thoughtfulness, "Because many times a 'room mom's' role is to work with and schedule the other parents. I choose to volunteer for the events in your classroom when I can share my time directly with you." He smiled and said, "Oh, I get it, Mom." He knew he was valued. Instead of running around trying to please everyone, I realized based upon my schedule and other priorities this decision was the best choice for me. Although I knew I would have enjoyed being a 'room mom', my other priorities were my focus.

As the years passed, this lesson of saying yes to myself gave me the time to serve on the board of directors for a nonprofit whose focus was to prepare inner city youth for college. I was grateful for this opportunity as it was a passion close to my heart. I was also fortunate to be a co-founder of a small nonprofit. Our mission was to help special needs children attend summer camp. These were my interests, so they came easier to me. There is not one path in life. There are many. If you can find what you love and enjoy, then you can create the time to pursue your passions. Time is limited. Follow what is in your heart.

This next life lesson I learned may provide someone a little more energy and peacefulness as they raise their children. At the time, I wanted to cry as this was happening. It now makes me laugh when I retell it. James was four years old and not behaving. I placed him in his room for a timeout. As soon as I put him into his room, he came out. This happened about 37 times! He came out 37 times. I put him back in. He came out. I'm serious. It was exhausting!! I was a young mom with full days, and it would have been easier to let him stay out; however, I learned over time that you communicate through your actions and follow-through. I knew he was not sick or in some sort of pain; he was just persistent and determined to test me. If I let him get his way this one time, it would have opened a door for disrespect.

Pick the most important lessons and be comfortable saying no to your children when it is a behavior lesson and not a safety or health concern. Doing this at an early age can help prevent challenges later in life when even more requests and demands come along. This will allow you to *say yes to you* and *have time for you*, while your children grow up well-behaved.

As simple as saying no can be, many people struggle with it. This is your nudge to think twice about how you choose to spend your time. You and your time are valuable. Say YES to you.

***

I am ready to politely say "no" so I can say YES to ME.

***

Actions I'm Choosing for My Best Self

- I will pick one area in my life where I feel overstretched and begin to say no to non-essential requests for my time.

- I will value my time and say YES to a passion in my heart.

Chapter 16
Release Your Guilt
and Take Care of YOU

"First take care of you;
then you can better care for those around you."
— Jackie Cantoni

How often do you try to be a superhero and "do it all" until you are exhausted, or your inner core and foundation begin to slowly crack? Now is the time to give yourself permission to re-energize.

Let's re-energize and rejuvenate you.

One common theme in *Are You Ready?* is placing yourself as a top priority in your life. Are you a priority? Especially as women, many times we put other people at the top of our priority list. We slowly sink to the bottom. As time passes, our energy and resilience become depleted. We may have less patience, cry more easily, and at times feel exhausted from the struggle.

In the previous chapters, you learned how to say *no* to activities not close to your heart and then schedule *Me Time*. These are strategies and steppingstones to take care of you. Now, as you begin to enjoy your interests and take care of yourself, consider this next strategy: *release the guilt*. Yes, release any guilt you may feel when you sprinkle in 10 to 20 minutes of *Me Time* each day. Let your focus be on your well-being and the benefit you will receive. As a bonus, when you are rejuvenated, you can then assist those around you, including your family, friends, and co-workers.

I learned this strategy I'll call *release the guilt* from my younger son, Nathan. As he was growing up, his different abilities required 100% care, seven days a week, 24 hours a day. At first it was very difficult for me to even consider time for myself. As I considered Nathan's needs, I felt a guilt associated with *Me Time.* However, as the days passed, I soon realized being worn down and exhausted benefitted no one, including Nathan or my family. I had to teach myself not to be a superhero and it was okay to let others assist in his care. As a mom, initially this was not easy for me. Over time, I learned to *release the guilt* and plan *Me Time.* This allowed me to take care of myself, become re-energized and, in turn, take better care of him. And Nathan continues to thank me with his contagious giggles.

It's a choice to take care of yourself. If you decide to relax on the couch and read for 10 minutes before starting dinner, that is okay. Allow this time to care for yourself. It doesn't have to be hours; it can be a 10-minute re-charge. A little bit of self-care sprinkled throughout your days can go a long way to energize your body and mind. If your family walks in and asks, "Hey, what are you doing? When is dinner?" you can graciously answer with confidence, "I need to recharge my batteries and am doing something for me first, so I can better take care of you."

In today's world this may sound selfish. However, it needs to happen. Interestingly, when you take care of yourself, you can become a role model and teach your children it is okay for them to take time and care for themselves.

I'll Be Napping

Why, as a society, are we so hesitant to say, "I took a nap" or "I did nothing today and enjoyed it"? As a culture that rushes from one activity to another, why do we not value the person who spent the weekend reading, taking a nap, or, when given a choice, spent time sitting, replenishing, and enjoying the beauty of silence?

"Having peace, happiness, and healthiness is my definition of beauty. And you can't have any of that without sleep."
— Beyoncé

Why is there often a stigma about down time? Even on vacation, we want to squeeze in so many activities we jokingly say we need a second vacation when we return home from the first vacation.

We often run ourselves down until we become sick and have no choice but to rest. Give yourself permission to "do nothing." This anonymous quote brings this technique to life, *"If you plan to do nothing, then doing nothing is not a waste of time."* Spending time alone with a good book or listening to music can regenerate and refresh you to be a better version of yourself.

Are You Ready?

Challenge yourself to pick 15 minutes this week and block off your calendar to do *"the nothing of your choice."*

Can you begin to slow down the pace of your life, take a breath, and maybe even take a re-energizing nap?

***

I am ready to release the guilt and take care of myself.

***

Actions I'm Choosing for My Best Self

- I will release my guilt as I focus on my well-being.

- I will choose a *taking care of me* activity each day — options include reading a book, taking a nap, taking a walk, or sitting in a warm bath.

- I will pick 15 minutes a week and block off my calendar to do "the nothing of my choice."

Chapter 17
"I'm So Busy"

"Sometimes you will never know the value of a moment,
until it becomes a memory."
— Dr. Seuss

Are your days filled with activities you love?

Or are you dashing from one activity to the next with "busyness" and losing focus on yourself? Are you overscheduled, yet not accomplishing what is in your heart?

As a society, we appear to be rushing through our day and losing much of our quality of life. "Oh, I'm so busy!" is something we hear when asking others, "How are you?" Many of us are going through the motions, but not really engaged.

Do you know people who believe the expression "I'm so busy" ties to some measure of significance? Is it a long to-do list? If anything, it wears you down, draining your energy from your true passions or priorities. I see it almost daily, many of us scurrying from one activity to the next with scattered focus.

It reminds me of the going out of business term "Chapter 11," when a company can go bankrupt from not concentrating on their priorities and goals. Can an "I'm so busy" day rob your time and take away focus from a larger priority sitting dormant in your heart?

Can you begin to distinguish between priorities and busyness? So, what does "I'm so busy" look like? Let's look further . . .

Here are some daily activities:

My Priority	"I'm So Busy"
Healthier eating and exercise	Surfing the Web
Relaxing and rejuvenating myself	Watching volumes of TV
Focusing on my career	Viewing others' online profiles
Family time and activities	Playing hours of video games
Giving back as a volunteer	Procrastinating or lacking focus
Launching a new passion	Overscheduling activities
Pursuing life-long learning	Inefficient use of my time by others

A technique to overcome "I'm so busy" is to follow your heart as you decide which activities should be filling your day. Are you excited about the opportunity? Is it something you look forward to? Would you wake up early or stay up late for it?

Now it is your turn to answer these questions for YOU. Take a moment and jot down your thoughts below. What are three priorities you can focus on and three "I'm so busy" activities you can diminish? For example:

1 My Priorities

Think about an activity you can *begin or continue,* such as cook a healthier meal, walk 20 minutes, or have lunch with a friend.

2 "I'm So Busy"

Think of an activity that you can *minimize or stop,* such as viewing others' online lives or playing fewer video games.

What are these for you?

My Priorities (focus on)	"I'm So Busy" (minimize/stop)
1.	1.
2.	2.
3.	3.

Are You Ready?

Are you ready to let go of busyness and concentrate on YOU?

Your goal is to reprioritize what is truly important and shift your focus to you and your top priorities. Let's have you has a top priority in your life.

***

I am ready to let go of busyness and focus on my priorities.

***

Actions I'm Choosing for My Best Self

- I will pick one area in my life where I am rushing through the motions and slow down to enjoy the moment.

- I will minimize or stop one "I'm so busy" activity.

- I will focus on a top priority.

Chapter 18
Really, a Banana?

"It's not whether you have the willpower,
it's whether you are ready to choose your best."
— Jackie Cantoni

Are you ready to be a healthier version of yourself?

Are you ready to have better health and well-being? It is not always about the willpower; it is about asking yourself whether you are ready to *choose* to be healthy. Once again, it's a choice you can make.

I laugh to myself when I think about how many people warn me to stay away from bananas because of the amount of carbs in them. What they are saying may very well be true. However, I enjoy bananas and eat them almost daily. It's likely bananas are not what is causing my weight fluctuations. It's enjoying more indulgent treats like ice cream, chocolate cream pie, and my mom's delicious Italian cooking.

Sometimes, we make things too complex in life. Really, a banana! Most of us know the secret formula to losing weight — eat fewer calories while making healthier selections and getting exercise. It's not a secret. However, our culture has made a multi-billion-dollar industry out of losing weight.

The reality is food is tempting, delicious, and, at times, comforting. It's also a big part of social occasions. After golf, we get a bite to eat. For a work event, we celebrate with food. Our gatherings with family and friends revolve around decadent dishes. It's difficult for many people to eat fewer calories, me included. There are so many tempting treats placed in front of us. Our choices are tested daily. . . in some cases, every hour.

You must decide if you want to make the choice to be a healthier version of yourself. It's a choice. You make the choice each day, each hour. At times, I choose my mom's eggplant parmigiana knowing it is not as healthy as something like a salad. The point is, I should not look to the diet industry for a quick fix to lose the weight I choose to put on from her delicious Italian cooking. I must own my decisions, then make the choice during the next meal or the next day to re-invest in who I am and want to be. It's not easy and that's where coaches and programs can add value. However, we know there is no quick fix.

If we are *better rested, take care of ourselves, and become a priority in our lives,* we can gain the internal strength to choose a healthier lifestyle. We all come in beautiful shapes and sizes. You can let your health be your guide.

The *Why* Behind Your Eating

Let's look at the *why* behind what you eat as well as the *triggers* causing you to eat. If you are run-down and tired, it's quicker and easier to grab a bagel than it is to make a salad. If you are worn out from not scheduling time for yourself, it's easier to plop on the couch with an unhealthy snack than go for a walk.

If you track the reasons *why* you eat throughout the day, you may be surprised how often you eat because you are simply tired or bored. Do you live to eat? Or eat to live?

Let's discover your *"why"* with these four triggers:

1. **Hungry and Nutritional**—a primary reason for eating.
   Here's what people may reach for:
   - Healthy greens, salads
   - Fruits and vegetables
   - Lean proteins
   - Nutritional grains

2. **Tired/Stressed/Rushing**—food is comforting.
   Here's what people may typically reach for and eat:
   - Ice cream (right out of the container!)
   - A drive-thru meal or some fast food before soccer
   - A quick meal when you arrive home tired
   - Salty or sugary snacks

3. **Bored**—you are looking for something to do and go to food.
   - Watching television and want a snack like popcorn
   - Open the cabinet and grab an unhealthy snack

4. **Social or Tempting**—you are with friends or family and indulge.
   - Appetizers with friends
   - Special holiday treats, like freshly baked cookies
   - Heavy meals

Are you Hungry, Tired/Stressed, Bored, or Social?

Fill in the four categories below with *what you ate during the past few days, why you ate it, and the time of day triggers.* This can help you discover eating patterns.

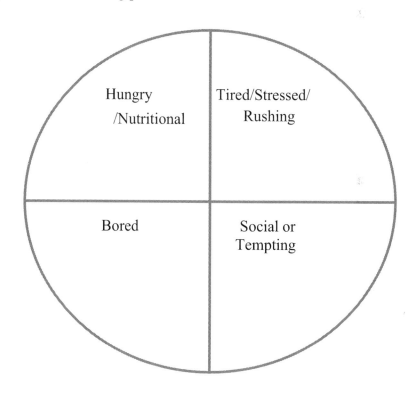

What and *why* I ate and the *time* of day.

Let's discover your *why* and more about YOU. What quadrant do you repeatedly fall within? Are you eating because you are truly hungry? Are you eating because you are dealing with a stressful situation? Or are you eating because you are bored or pressed for time rushing to an appointment or a soccer game?

You may find yourself in a social setting where there are appetizers, desserts, and drinks, and it is much easier to eat when delicious and tempting options are placed in front of you. You know eating a candy bar may not be the best choice, so what is the real reason *why* you eat it? Did you visit the vending machine because your conversation with your boss or co-worker did not go well? Are you sitting on an airplane, bored and trying to pass the time? What is your eating trigger?

The answer to your *why* can be a root cause. It can be a barrier you want to identify. Once you understand your barriers or obstacles to losing weight, then you can begin strategies to address them.

If you schedule *"me time"* when you get a stress craving, it may help to stay ahead of that trigger.

As a strategy, if you get tired or stressed each afternoon at work or school, instead of going to the vending machine, plan to bring in a healthier, more satisfying snack you will enjoy. I bring a banana with me. You choose.

Let's look at how tracking your *why* and *triggers* may help.

Leap Over Your Triggers to Care for You

Just for today, select one food or drink you plan to eliminate. One item, one day. And let's also pick one major trigger point. For example, "I will not eat standing at the counter when I get home tired from work." Of course, always check with your doctor, as necessary.

Jot this down for you . . .

I choose not to eat/drink _____ *today.*

I choose to replace it with a healthier choice, like _____.

You may say to yourself, *"I work hard, and I deserve to eat this treat."* Ironically, the opposite may be true — you work hard, therefore you deserve to take care of yourself and your body.

Habits may take a month or more to even begin to become part of your normal routine. That can be a long time, if staring at a plate of broccoli is not one of your favorite activities. With the *why* and *triggers*, you can be more conscious of your food and health choices. One step at a time.

Remember, you are no longer only *trying* your best; you are now *choosing* your best. Choose to eat less volume and make healthier choices for the long term. Your choice. It is a mindset shift from thinking, *"I feel deprived because I cannot have this"* to a new way of thinking, *"I choose to be healthy and no longer want to have this."*

Now is your time to take care of you. Choose to make healthier life choices for a healthier version of you. Choose YOU.

***

I am ready to be a healthier version of myself.

***

Actions I'm Choosing for My Best Self

- I will identify my *why* and *triggers* to discover my eating pattern.

- I will select one food or drink I plan to eliminate.

- I will pick one trigger and replace it with a healthier plan.

- I will realize a well-cared for ME will have more energy and discipline to make better health choices.

Chapter 19
Pay Yourself First

*"Too many people spend money they haven't earned
to buy things they don't need,
to impress people they don't like."*
—Will Smith

Are you ready to take care of yourself, financially?

Your financial well-being is not always about the amount of money you make; it's often about the amount of money you save and invest in yourself and your future.

There is something about financial security that can be central to your overall health and happiness. This kind of financial reassurance is freeing. It helps you relax so you can focus on your purpose at hand. Uncertainty of your resources can be stressful and distracting as it weighs on your mind.

On your journey to your best self, one empowering and foundational financial strategy is to *pay yourself first*. By paying yourself, you are placing money upfront each month into a savings account for your future. It is making yourself a priority. Up until now, you may spend or pay your bills first and then if there is any money left over, save. Can you shift your thinking and begin to manage your savings upfront, along with your bills?

My dad taught me this simple strategy — to save upfront — when I was eleven years old. He started with my allowance and would encourage me to place a portion into a savings account each week. I would ride my bike to the bank to save. Then he would often surprise me at the end of the month and match any money I chose to save that month. I am grateful for this life lesson and skill that my dad taught me when I was a young girl.

For your first step, select an amount or a percentage of your income. Even starting with $10, $25, $100, or $1,000 a month to get you going is a great beginning. You can smile and feel good inside as you begin investing in yourself. Based upon your resources, challenge yourself, regardless of your level of income. At the beginning of the month, allocate an amount upfront into your savings as you pay your bills. If helpful, *choose* to say no to a non-necessity purchase. Ask yourself, do I really need this? *Paying yourself first* is a habit you want to develop early in life.

Think about one of your financial goals. Do you want to start your own business, take golf lessons, retire, or further your education, which will require financial funding? What is this priority for you? Once you identify your goal, choose to make it intentional:

My Financial Goal:

I will save $_____ (dollars) per month.

This savings will be for my _____ goal or priority.

My timeline to achieve my financial goal is by _____.

Are You Ready?

Make YOU a priority and invest in yourself. Set your financial goal and then inch by inch, choose you and achieve it.

***

I am ready to plan financially to achieve my goal.

***

Actions I'm Choosing for My Best Self

- I will identify a goal that requires financial resources.

- I will select a dollar amount and each month pay myself first — upfront along with my bills.

- I will add monthly to my savings account and watch it grow.

- I will be grateful as I invest in myself.

Part Three Take-Aways
You Matter . . . Make Yourself a Priority

*Simple treasures to nudge you on your journey
to becoming the best version of yourself.*

- Choose to be the healthiest version of you. It's a choice.

- Focus on *why* you eat, the triggers, and the strategies to choose a healthier you.

- Be a top priority in your life.

- Release the guilt.

- Create a *Me List*.

- Begin with 20 minutes a day creating the *7 Days of YOU*.

- Graciously say *no* to an activity not close to your heart.

- Say YES to you, your priorities, and passions.

- Encourage yourself to slow down.

- Embrace the idea "I'm so busy" is not a badge of honor.

- Give yourself permission to "do nothing."

- Pay yourself first.

Are You Ready?

Part Four

Be Positively Contagious

Part Four: Introduction
Be Positively Contagious

You'll learn how to:

- ❖ Be an inspirational leader.

- ❖ Reflect on how daily actions can influence your attitude.

- ❖ Share your enthusiasm and confidence with others.

- ❖ *Pop open* and be positively contagious.

- ❖ Sprinkle in laughter. Plan to laugh, really belly laugh.

- ❖ Let your optimistic attitude create new opportunities.

- ❖ Quiet your mind to discover what is in your heart.

- ❖ Release the weight of the world from your shoulders.

- ❖ Forgive yourself.

- ❖ Be grateful and count your blessings. . . starting with you.

- ❖ Create lasting memories as part of your legacy.

- ❖ Remember you, too, are a beautiful swan.

Jackie Cantoni

Chapter 20
Laugh at Yourself

"I love people who make me laugh. I honestly think it is the thing I like most, to laugh. It's probably the most important thing in a person."
— Audrey Hepburn

Laugh at yourself. Smile. Smile more. Keep smiling. Give your smile away. I have a saying, *"When you smile at someone, if they don't smile back, then they needed your smile more than you."*

At times, we may take ourselves too seriously. Can you give yourself and others the gift of laughter?

When I think of laughter, I think of Ellen DeGeneres. Ellen is naturally entertaining and funny. She followed her passion and discovered her purpose in life — she brings laughter to others. Her purpose is simple and significant at the same time. Ellen loves to make others laugh . . .

"Never follow anyone else's path,
unless you're in the woods and you're lost, and you see a path.
Then by all means follow that path."
— Ellen DeGeneres

Do you take laughter for granted? My husband came home from a lunch with a 90-year-old friend. When I asked, "How was your lunch?" his response was, "She recommended watching funny movies and television shows that make you laugh. She talked about the *importance of laughter in one's life.*" Priceless advice and I couldn't agree more!

My dad, sister Diane, and son James are remarkable at adding laughter to my days — you know, the belly laughter where sometimes you cannot even breathe because you are laughing so hard. Have you ever laughed so hard you couldn't even catch your breath? Imagine what would happen if you could bottle this great energy and feel-good mood. Well, why not choose to re-create and re-introduce the power of laughter into your days.

As a personal challenge, pick a day and highlight laughter — draw attention to making yourself or others laugh. Plan to laugh out loud. Belly laugh. Humor is so essential that it is okay if it is not always spontaneous. It can be sharing a funny story, reading a joke, or for me, being entertained by a comedian.

Take a moment to jot down below how you will bring laughter to your day.

I will plan to do_____and enjoy a good laugh.

Are You Ready?

Laughter is a gift you give yourself and others. Humor is a secret formula to happiness and well-being.

Interestingly, as you spread laughter, you will also get it sprinkled back onto you. Maybe it is true, laughter is the best medicine.

***

I am ready to add laughter to my days.

***

Actions I'm Choosing for My Best Self

- I will remember to bring laughter into my days.

- I will laugh each day to help release the weight of the world from my shoulders.

- I will seek out laughter to fill my spirit with new energy.

Chapter 21
Be Positively Contagious

"As a leader, one of the things that's most important
is to know your team needs to see you as confident."
— Steve Kerr, Coach Golden State Warriors

Emotions and energy are contagious. When you are leading or motivating others, such as a teammate, spouse, child, or sales prospect, your emotions can influence the results. Confidence is contagious, as is fear or lack of belief in yourself. Lack of conviction can be felt. As a leader, how can you inspire your team or family? Can you be positively engaging while displaying confidence at work, school, or at home?

Pop Open with Enthusiasm and Inspiration

One of my favorite foods at festivals is kettle corn. It is a delicious, mouth-watering, sweet, and salty popcorn. This popcorn reminds me of people. Sometimes your outlook can be sweet. You can be supportive, kind, grateful, or generous as you move through your days, creating positivity for yourself and others. Other times, your emotions can be salty. These are the moments when you are less flexible or lack inspiration. Either way, your tone and mood can be positively or negatively contagious to those around you.

Are You Ready?

Let's discover the atmosphere you create when you are interacting with others. In the next section jot down the times you fed your mind with optimistic actions and thoughts. How often did you have an upbeat effect on a conversation or another person? Did you create an uplifting mood for those around you? In the bottom section, write when you felt stuck, out of balance, or influenced by adverse media making you feel less than positively contagious.

Positive
Jot down today's positive attitudes, mood, action, deeds.

Negative
Jot down today's negative attitudes, mood, actions, deeds.

Are you positively contagious? Consider your responses and the aura you create with those around you. As you reflect on yourself as a leader, spouse, schoolmate, or parent, begin to challenge yourself and replay your interaction in your mind.

Can you turn any negative interactions into opportunities to spread positivity and inspiration?

Positive Energy You *Receive* from Others

Similarly, others' dispositions and energy can have a positive or negative influence on you. Have you ever noticed some people leave you feeling energized, whereas other individuals can leave you exhausted, completely drained of energy? You want to be mindful of your interactions and choose to surround yourself with optimistic and inspirational people.

If you find yourself surrounded by negative people or in uncomfortable situations, then move along. These can cause you to spiral into self-doubt or move you to make unfavorable choices. Choose to walk away and not let someone else's negativity sway your attitude or your decisions.

As a reflection strategy:

1 Identify one or more people in your life who elicit positive energy and fill your spirit with encouragement and an optimistic outlook:

_____

_____

2 Think to yourself of one or more people in your life who elicit negative energy, drain your spirit, and have you questioning your own judgement.

Others daily energy can surely influence your drive, motivation, and future success. At times, you may need to reach deep within yourself to find your leading source of positive inspiration and motivation.

Have you ever thought, "If only my (think of who to yourself) were more supportive?" *For example:* friends, family, or co-workers. If you currently do not have the support you need at work, home, or school, then consider seeking out a supportive mentor to inspire you. A positively contagious attitude for yourself and those who surround you is an essential key on your journey to your best self.

Are You Crusty?

Over time, if you do not intentionally focus on bringing positivity into your life, you can develop a crusty outer shell. Just like popcorn can grow stale, so can your optimism. You may let the world or your circumstances negatively influence you and take away your core of kindness. What's the point of that? As you journey through your life, be careful not to develop a crusty, hard outer shell. Be like popcorn . . . pop open and then *choose* to be inspiring, optimistic, and positively contagious.

***

I am ready to be positively contagious.

***

Actions I'm Choosing for My Best Self

- I will create contagious positive energy that attracts people and opportunities to me.

- I will surround myself with uplifting people as others' energy can influence my motivation and future success.

- I will *pop open* and choose to be inspiring and optimistic.

Chapter 22
Forgive Yourself
and Reclaim Your Energy

"It's not always easy, however dig deep and choose to forgive."
— Jackie Cantoni

Have you ever said something socially or professionally and then wished you could take back your words? Have you ever been told unkind words that linger in your mind and take away your energy?

When you hold a grudge against someone or yourself for doing something you perceive as "wrong," you hold yourself and your feelings captive. You remain upset and give away your happiness.

This is also true as you think about *forgiving yourself when a conversation or your performance did not go as planned.*

One strategy for forgiving yourself or others is to realize you are hurting not only yourself by holding on to this feeling, but also hurting those you care about. By this I mean, if you are unforgiving and critical of yourself, you are no longer sharing your joy and laughter with those around you. You are taking away from the lives of others — many times, those you love.

109

One technique for allowing forgiveness is to address the concern head on. Here are two examples:

Scenario 1 — Have you ever felt the following?

"I continue to hold onto the unfavorable words my boss (or teacher) mentioned to me about my performance on a recent project. Her message plays repeatedly in my mind and is draining my energy."

As one way to forgive yourself, step back and look in the rearview mirror. Then address the concern head on and release the negative energy. For example, you can say something like:

"I forgive myself. I did the best I could with the project information I had at the time. I take ownership for my actions. Next time I will invest more time in the project. I am at peace knowing I learned from this experience. I forgive myself and will refocus my energy to create a new opportunity."

Scenario 2 — Have you ever felt the following?

"My peer was unkind and spoke unpleasant words that stung my soul."

To forgive another person, you can say to yourself:

I forgive (peer). Her unkind way is a reflection on her and not on me. She may be carrying hurtfulness in her heart. She tried to make herself feel better at the expense of me. I wish her well and will be moving on. I will refocus my energy on me and one of my priorities. I choose me.

Are You Ready?

Forgiveness at times can be difficult; however, holding on robs you of your happiness. Give yourself the gift of forgiveness.

Select one area in your life that you have been holding onto with disappointment:

_____

_____

_____

Jot down how you plan to forgive and release this negative recurring thought pattern:

_____

_____

_____

_____

_____

Although you may think your disappointment in yourself is yours and affecting only you, often this is not the case. The joy you should be bringing to the world is missing. Instead of holding on, repurpose your energy, forgive, and spread your love onto yourself and others.

***

I am ready to forgive myself or others and repurpose my energy.

***

Actions I'm Choosing for My Best Self

- I will forgive myself and others who may have hurt me.

- I will select one area in my life that I have been holding onto with disappointment. I will address the concern, forgive, and release it.

- I will realize forgiveness repurposes my energy for myself and those I love.

Chapter 23
Refill Your Heart

"I am grateful for what I am and have. My Thanksgiving is perpetual."
— Henry David Thoreau

Count your blessings . . .

Being grateful can fill your heart and life with positivity, purpose, and loving energy. As you encounter unappreciative situations or stressful days, this love and energy can be drained causing you, at times, to feel sadness. I have seen many people, especially young adults, become withdrawn as they view other's lives and lose sight of their uniqueness, talent, and beauty. As a result, they may unknowingly become ungrateful for what they have and who they are. The opposite can also be true. By showing appreciation and gratitude for who you are and your gifts, you can re-fill your heart, generate positive energy, uplift your mood, and your life.

Try this . . . think of the first three things that come to mind for which you are grateful . . .

"Why I Am Grateful"

1. _____

2. _____

3. _____

How does it make you feel? Did you smile?

I think of gratitude as a key that unlocks the door to a joyful spirit. When days go by without gratefulness, the door can feel stuck, causing an emptiness inside. The door becomes un-wedged and reopens once you re-focus on what you are grateful for. If you have draining days, reach deep within your heart and re-introduce gratitude to refill your spirit with joy.

Let's mindfully pause and think about how you can fill your days with gratitude. Here we go again, more time to invest in YOU. Below, reflect on what and who you are grateful for in your life. Continue your *Why I am Grateful* list and identify your top ten things or people.

An example of what is on my list: I am grateful to have running water. Why does that sound strange? Well, today the central water pipe at our house burst and water began shooting out. The water was gushing out of the pipe! To quickly stop the waterflow, we shut off the main control valve to our home. Now, not only did we have a broken pipe, we had another concern: NO running water. After spending the day without running water and feeling the inconvenience that brings, I would now add *having a working water supply* to my *Why I Am Grateful* list.

Interestingly, I may not have even considered water on my list. It reminded me that sometimes I take things for granted. Is there anything or anyone you take for granted and can be grateful for?

Count your blessings and start with YOU!

Are You Ready?

Alright, it's your turn to continue . . .

"Why I Am Grateful"

4. _____

5. _____

6. _____

7. _____

8. _____

9. _____

10. _____

Bonus.... What else are you grateful for? Can you add five more?

11. _____

12. _____

13. _____

14. _____

15. _____

On days when you need an extra pick-me-up, you can refer to this list and smile.

***

I am ready to be grateful and refill my heart with joy.

***

Actions I'm Choosing for My Best Self

- I will jot down 15 *Why I Am Grateful* items and state them aloud.

- I will have a grateful moment each day and be thankful for all that I do have in the moment.

- I will remember gratitude is a key that unlocks the door to a joyful spirit.

Chapter 24
What if You Were Granted a Redo?

"The door is wide and open, don't go back to sleep."
— Rumi

If you could live each day twice without anyone else knowing about it, how would the repeated day be different? What if you passed on and then were given a second chance to come back to relive your life? Would you slow down? Would you be more attentive? Would you worry less because you already knew the outcome?

Let's pick a day or an event and have you approach it as if the day already occurred and you are reliving it. What would you do with an opportunity for a "re-do"? How would you handle it? Would your attitude or perspective be different?

Would you hug a little tighter given a second chance?

Would you turn off your cellphone to enjoy quality time with someone?

Would your reactions to the "small stuff" diminish?

This is a mindset shift to help you *slow down, be grateful, and appreciate your life.* If you had a second chance at life, would you fill your days with more gratitude, kindness, and attentiveness?

***

I am ready to live as if I had a "redo" of my day.

***

Actions I'm Choosing for My Best Self

- I will pick one person each day and let them know why I appreciate them.

- I will slow down and appreciate the little things in my life.

Chapter 25
Silence

"Silence is a source of great strength."
— Lao Tzu

Are you comfortable with silence?

How about when talking or interacting with others — do you feel the need to fill the empty silence?

In college, I had to give a speech as one of the assignments for a public speaking class. Before selecting the topic, I asked the professor if it would be okay to speak on the influence of silence in a conversation. I mentioned to him that I would begin the presentation with 30 seconds of silence. He agreed.

So, I walked up to the podium, looked up at the audience and stood silently staring back at them. At first the audience was patient. Then, after 10 or 15 seconds, the audience became uncomfortable. People were squirming in their seats, looking at each other for answers. They appeared to be uneasy with the silence. After the 30-second void of silence passed, I started my presentation with the word "silence." It was impactful to see how many of us can be uncomfortable with silence. How comfortable are you with silence in a conversation, interview, or even at home?

119

The point is, it is okay to have quiet in your life. Or a silent pause when talking with others. As a lesson learned, feel comfortable not filling every void with some form of "noise" in your life. After all, it may be true that *"Silence is golden."*

As a first technique to harness silence, schedule time to *sit quietly and reflect on you* and what makes you happy. Release your thoughts and reflect on what you hold in your heart. When worry and internal noise swirl in your mind, either plan an action step or choose to let it go. Then repurpose your energy on a true priority.

You may need to quiet your mind to hear what is in your heart. Treat yourself to quiet time.

***

I am ready to quiet my mind and hear what is in my heart.

***

Actions I'm Choosing for My Best Self

- I will quiet my mind to discover what is resting in my heart.

- I will address one worry swirling repeatedly in my head.

- I will let silence fit comfortably into a conversation or interaction with others.

Chapter 26
The Swan

"The confidence you instill in children
can change the world."
— Jackie Cantoni

Comedian Amy Schumer jokingly responded to an *InStyle* magazine question regarding her childhood, *"My parents made me think I was a genius supermodel and it was kind of too late when I found out that they had been lying."*

I quickly related to this quote as my parents and sister made me feel like a "beautiful swan" as a child. When I look back on my middle school years with braces and a chubby face, I recall always feeling beautiful and talented. My parents and sister continue to fill my soul with kind words of encouragement.

The truth is we believe what we hear over and over. Instilling self-confidence is crucial when you are raising children or encouraging a friend. I'm not suggesting false hope or fake praise; rather, I mean instilling a sense of self-belief and beauty no matter what you look like.

Can you begin to surround yourself with others who love, appreciate, and inspire you to be the best version of yourself? If you do not yet have others as your champions, you may need to reach deep within yourself to draw upon your inner strength and recognize your own beauty. At times, just as we must instill self-confidence in children, we must also instill self-confidence and inner belief in ourselves.

You are talented, beautiful, and your uniqueness is a gift. Focus on your strengths and the unique gifts you bring to the world each day. Let your inner light shine. Choose to believe in YOU.

Remember you, too, are *a beautiful swan.*

***

I am ready to recognize my own beauty.

***

Actions I'm Choosing for My Best Self

- I will surround myself with others who love, appreciate, and inspire me.

- I will inspire myself and remember what I love about myself from Chapter 2.

- I will look in the mirror and see my own uniqueness, talents and beauty.

Chapter 27
The Letter with Love and a Legacy

"Create memories to last more than one lifetime."
— Jackie Cantoni

Are you intentionally creating memories, traditions, and a legacy?

Staying in touch with those I care about is important to me. So, when Robin, a family friend, shared her story of how her father wrote to her at college and the impact it had on her, I was inspired. When our son James was about to go off to college, I set a goal to write a letter to him each week for the four years he would be away at school.

On Sunday evening I would start my "Dear James" letter with smiley faces and hearts, then write about the week that passed and what we were looking forward to the week ahead. I included two or three inspirational quotes. Each week, I placed $20 in the envelope. I thought a little college spending money would be appreciated by a young man living the "college life." I also knew these little things would give him something extra to look forward to each week as he received my letter.

Four years later, when he was about to graduate, I wrote the culminating college letter. I shared how proud his dad and I were of him and how he has been a treasure in our lives. The usual one-page letter was transformed into eight pages, with pictures from his first school bus ride through his college years. I placed the envelope on his chair at graduation. After the graduation celebration, as our family packed up the boxes from his dorm room, I realized he still had his stack of letters from Mom. Wow! James had saved each one. The feeling in my heart was that James realized the four years of letters were labors of love from a mom to her son.

Positive memories and keepsakes are what can fill your heart with happiness and bring added joy to your life. The reason this college writing goal was achieved was because I completed one letter at a time. If I had set out to write more than 100 letters, I may have failed. So, I began step by step and inch by inch to accomplish something that now is a special keepsake and fond memory.

What are a few ways you can create lasting memories or traditions with your family, friends, or in your community?

1. _____

2. _____

3. _____

Life is a collection of our memories and experiences. These traditions can bring comfort and joy to your days and to those you care about. Memories give you energy and make for a meaningful life. These memories are part of your legacy.

When James grows much older and shares his life stories from his rocking chair, chances are he will tell about the many letters of inspiration his mom sent to him each week at college and the influence they had on his school days. That's part of my legacy.

Your legacy is a gift you give to others. So, why not give others your best self?

**

I am ready to create lasting memories, part of my legacy.

**

Actions I'm Choosing for My Best Self

- I will plan to create a tradition or memories to leave as part of my legacy.

- I will remember a legacy is a gift I give myself and others.

Part Four Take-Aways
Be Positively Contagious

*Simple treasures to nudge you on your journey
to becoming the best version of yourself.*

🐝 Be positively contagious.

🐝 Pop open with renewed energy.

🐝 Plan to laugh . . . belly laugh.

🐝 Let gratitude unlock the door to a joyful spirit.

🐝 Be thankful for the gifts you have in the moment.

🐝 Forgive yourself and others for imperfections.

🐝 Approach your life as if you were given a second chance.

🐝 Let silence quiet your mind to hear what is in your heart.

🐝 Leave a legacy of memories to share with others.

🐝 Remember you, too, are a beautiful swan.

🐝 Count your blessing and start with YOU!

Are You Ready?

Part Five

HOW to Get There

Part Five: Introduction
HOW to Get There

You'll learn how to:

- ❖ Do more of what makes you happy.

- ❖ Uncover a passion in your heart.

- ❖ Be guided step-by-step to achieve your passion.

- ❖ Release negative self-chatter and self-doubt.

- ❖ Overcome obstacles and fears.

- ❖ Approach your goals one step at a time as you check off and celebrate each milestone.

- ❖ Learn strategies on HOW to make an idea come to life.

- ❖ Bring inspiration and a new spark to your days.

- ❖ Celebrate you, because you *are* enough.

- ❖ Discover a world of endless possibilities.

- ❖ Embrace the thought of success.

- ❖ *Stick your neck out* to succeed.

Jackie Cantoni

Chapter 28
Inch by Inch

"The journey of a thousand miles must begin with a single step."
— Lao Tzu

How many people get overwhelmed by a large initiative? They may put off their true passions or even smaller projects because they don't know where to start.

Since I was a young girl, another quote that I live by is, *"Inch by inch, life's a cinch. Yard by yard, life is hard."* The unknown author provides a foundational strategy to attain goals with the simple and easier, "inch by inch" and step-by-step approach to tackling even the most complex projects.

When faced with a task, challenge, or opportunity at work, school, or home, remember to approach it by asking, "What is the first 'step or inch' to advance forward?"

In Chapter 33, you will pick a priority and together we will walk through the steps inch by inch to move your idea forward.

When you tackle a goal, passion, or project in bite size pieces, your results will accumulate, and you will find your goals can be easier to achieve. It's simple, yet how many times do you put off a goal as it can appear unattainable at first glance?

Jot down one goal you plan to approach in bite size pieces:

_____

This even works when you dream BIG. At times, BIG dreams can be overwhelming or intimidating; the key is to act in small steps. Then, once you have momentum, you can move forward at your pace. Remember to celebrate and be grateful — one step at a time.

*The inch-by-inch strategy also applies if in the past you sabotaged yourself by thinking you are not enough — not good enough, not rich enough, not thin enough. One of the keys to the "inch" is celebrating each step because each step **is** enough as you choose your best self. You are enough.* **Remember to love being you, inch by inch.**

***

I am ready to tackle and achieve my goals, inch by inch.

***

Actions I'm Choosing for My Best Self

- I will approach my goal one step at a time and be appreciative for each small accomplishment.

- I will celebrate as I move toward my dreams inch by inch and step-by-step.

Chapter 29
Think Like the Tortoise

"Like the tortoise, stick your neck out to succeed."
— Jackie Cantoni

Do you remember the fable of the "Tortoise and the Hare?" This famous tale by Aesop has been used for generations to teach a life lesson. I'd like to offer that the tortoise was a girl . . . sure of herself and steady. The tortoise is confident in each step she takes to reach the finish line. She achieves her goal. Slow but steady, she wins the race. You go, girl!!

While standing at the starting gate and about to take her first step, how easy would it have been for the tortoise to look up and see the rabbit sprint out ahead of her, and give up? She could have been telling herself, "I'm not fast enough. I'm not good enough. Look how fast the rabbit is. I don't have a chance." *Have you ever done this and doubted yourself and your abilities?*

The tortoise was wise enough to know the race was truly not against the rabbit. She wanted to finish for herself. She stuck her neck out and took the first step.

Like the tortoise, we all must realize our journey is our own. We must look internally for self-discipline. So, what do you want to pursue, yet have been afraid to stick your neck out to accomplish?

As an example, is there a telephone call you want to make but have put off because you're afraid? Or an introduction to someone new that you have been hesitant to pursue? Look internally for the courage to take the first step.

As you take your first step on your journey, you may meet Guides and Naysayers. A Guide may offer insight or assist with identifying and overcoming barriers, whereas a Naysayer may only develop doubt in your mind. When you come across Naysayers, think like a tortoise and politely step forward to pass those who doubt your abilities. Remember the rabbit who, at each stop along the way, would zip by and try to discourage the tortoise in her journey? The rabbit, through his actions, would remind the tortoise: "Tortoises are slow. Tortoises can't win a race." Do you encounter people who behave like the rabbit? Their unsupportive actions make you feel inferior. Let go of those negative feelings and realize it's their issue, not yours.

As Eleanor Roosevelt reminds us, *"No one can make you feel inferior without your consent."* Next time you encounter someone who dismisses your positive efforts like the rabbit, smile to yourself, turn, and take the first step in the other direction — the direction of your heart. Remember to think like the tortoise and cross the finish line to achieve your goal.

***

I am ready to think like a tortoise
and stick my neck out to achieve my goal.

***

Actions I'm Choosing for My Best Self

- I will have self-discipline, sure and steady like the tortoise.

- I will step in the other direction if I encounter Naysayers.

- I will believe in myself and "stick my neck out" to pursue my passion and goals.

Chapter 30
Ask HOW

*"Empty pockets never held anyone back.
Only empty heads and empty hearts can do that."*
— Norman Vincent Peale

Do you often talk yourself out of pursuing a new idea?

You may experience this when you fill your mind with excuses of having no time, resources, or belief in yourself. You can find yourself thinking of the reasons *why* something may not work.

One strategy to overcome your self-doubt is to focus on three simple letters . . . HOW.

If you are pursuing a new project, innovative idea, or career advancement and find your head filling with reasons why your idea may not work, immediately shift your thinking and ask HOW.

The "how" can move you from a negative to a positive thought pattern. Then you can let the concept develop and plan the action steps to achieve your goal. If others are concentrating on *why something may not work,* pivot the conversation and ask HOW to move the idea forward.

Are You Ready?

Think of one of your goals or innovative ideas. Ask yourself, *HOW do I move this idea forward?* Jot down the first step:

_____

Remember one step at a time to move you closer to your goal.

So how did I learn about the "how strategy"? My husband, Jim, taught me to ask HOW and "let an idea grow." For years, on the wall in his office he displayed the three letters HOW. Jim learned this type of technique a couple of decades ago at a Brian Tracy seminar and shared it with me. I am grateful to have come across this life lesson.

How simple is asking HOW? Yet, it can be powerful as you watch your ideas bloom along with your confidence.

***

I am ready to focus on HOW to make an idea work.

***

Actions I'm Choosing for My Best Self

- I will be open to exploring new ideas.

- I will ask HOW and identify the first action step.

- I will focus on HOW to let an idea grow.

Chapter 31
Three Fears to Leap

"Anyone who has never made a mistake
has never tried anything new."
— Albert Einstein

Overcoming fear is an essential key to start living your dream life.

Sometimes fears stem within your mind like negative self-chatter and self-doubt. Other times, barriers can be related to resources such as not having the time, money, or family support.

One impactful strategy to overcome obstacles is to clearly identify them upfront. Sometimes the unknown is more frightening than the known. If you admit in writing that you do not know the rules to play golf and are afraid to walk onto a golf course, then you can begin the steps to overcome that one fear.

You need to acknowledge your obstacles and fears so you can move past them.

Let's tackle some fears . . .

A First Fear

Failure is inevitable. Accept it and move on.

One of the greatest barriers to achievement seems to be fear of failure caused by self-doubt. At times, you may subconsciously choose not to set priorities. You may be anxious and feel you cannot achieve them. Whenever you are faced with self-doubt or fear of failure, remember this quote from Roger W. Babson, the Founder of Babson College: *"It is wise to keep in mind that neither success nor failure is ever final."* Failure is truly a steppingstone to success. Failure is only telling you *this way may not work; let's choose a different approach.*

Fear of failure can be paralyzing. It can stop you before you even start. To overcome your fears, begin to practice this 3-step technique:

1) **Write down** your fears or obstacles. Clearly identify each one.

2) Focus on **HOW** to overcome them. *Ask how.*

3) Then identify **one action step at a time** to advance forward.

What is one step you can take to create momentum?

If your goal is a new work position, then take the first step of updating your resume. There is no risk in this one step, and it moves you forward, creating momentum at your own pace. As you check off each step, you become closer to achieving your goal.

A Second Fear
"I have no time."

A second barrier when planning to fulfill a passion or purpose is *the misperception of "I have no time."* The reality is there is often enough time to do what's genuinely important to you, so release the mindset of "I don't have time" and *refocus on you and your priorities. There is enough time, if you choose to invest it in yourself.*

Remember, move forward one inch or action step at a time, at your own pace. Each step, regardless of how small, can advance you, even if it is only 15 minutes a day to start. If a goal is truly important to you, then choose to schedule 15 minutes of *Me Time.*

At the end of your life's journey, what do you want to say you did with your time?

A Third Fear
"What if . . . I actually accomplish my goal?"

Michelangelo inspires us to reach higher with his life accomplishments and words of wisdom, *"The greater danger for most of us lies not in setting our aim too high and falling short; but in setting our aim too low and achieving our mark."*

A third barrier is, "What if I actually accomplish my goal? How will I handle the success?" Deep down, do you fear being successful? On the surface, you may think, "of course not!"

However, what does success look like, and would you be comfortable with the change of a new lifestyle? It's a mindset shift and habit to embrace the thought of success. Believe in yourself. *You can handle what life gives you . . . Why not handle success?*

> *"You can't be that kid standing at the top of the waterslide over-thinking. You have to go down the chute."*
> —Tina Fey

Embrace the thought of success and allow this excitement and energy to advance you forward in the direction of your dreams.

***

I am ready to overcome my fears.

***

Actions I'm Choosing for My Best Self

- I will write down my fears, then address them one action step at a time.

- I will make myself a priority, schedule *Me Time,* and overcome the obstacle of "I have no time."

- I will welcome success.

Chapter 32
Conquer Negative Self-Chatter

*"Self-doubt can create fatigue in your mind, whereas
focused action can create achievement in your life."*
— Jackie Cantoni

How often do we defeat ourselves before even trying?

Conquering negative self-chatter and self-doubt is an interwoven thread throughout *Are You Ready?* In earlier chapters we covered strategies on overcoming negative self-chatter. It now deserves additional focus thanks to the overwhelming influence it can have on your journey to your best self. If you choose to surmount this one obstacle, you can discover a key to happier days. As you let go of self-doubt, you will advance forward and propel toward success.

Think about your goals — how often does self-doubt swirl in your mind or negative self-chatter frolic in your head, causing you to shift your focus to *why* something *may not work*?

Overcoming self-doubt is a life skill. As with any skill, it may take practice. Starting today, as you focus on your life, can you apply the techniques in this chapter to help eliminate self-doubt and negative self-chatter?

Are You Ready?

Here are examples of negative self-chatter and self-doubt.

1. Have you ever looked in the mirror and criticized one of your features? The words *"my hair always looks messy and dry,"* can create negativity and drain your energy.

   Instead, when you look in the mirror, focus on a feature you love about yourself, like your beautiful smile. Acknowledge your smile, then take the first action step to concentrate on your hair. Ask yourself, "How do I fix my hair?" Then *let "action" replace your negative self-chatter.* Your action step can be as simple as buying a new hairbrush, researching different conditioners, or possibly changing your diet. This momentum can create a solution or positive energy to re-focus you.

   Begin to replace unproductive thoughts with action. It's a simple strategy, yet how often does negative self-chatter consume your thoughts or deplete your energy?

2. Or how about when you think of a new "out of the box" idea at work, school, or home and your first reaction is *"that will never work!"* This initial negative reaction may allow self-doubt to automatically seep into your thoughts.

   Instead, begin to practice the technique of asking HOW. *How can I move this idea forward?* What one step will create positive momentum? Plan the first step. Then the second step. One step at a time moving toward your goal.

Now it is your turn. Jot down a time when you have reoccurring negative self-chatter:

I usually tell myself: _____

_____

_____

I will remove this negative self-chatter or self-doubt. I will replace it with (insert optimistic thoughts and/or a first action step):

_____

_____

_____

"Faith is taking the first step
even when you can't see the whole staircase."
— Martin Luther King, Jr.

Can you find the faith and belief in yourself to take the first step without seeing the whole staircase?

When self-doubt seeps in, *choose to swap your thoughts with action. Focus on HOW to make an idea work, and the action steps to drive success. One step at a time.* Then whisper to yourself, *I Got This!*

Here's a summary of some of the foundational tools in your *Are You Ready?* toolbox to overcome negative self-chatter:

1. Be intentional. Write down your goal.

2. Identify the thoughts causing self-doubt or self-chatter.

3. Ask HOW to overcome obstacles and move the goal forward.

4. Start with three "today I choose to" action statements.

5. *Create the steps to swap negative thoughts with positive action.*

6. Take the first step to create momentum.

7. Make yourself a priority.

8. Focus one day at a time.

9. Believe in yourself. Replace self-doubt with positive self-talk.

10. Share your voice and ask others for help or guidance.

11. Stay in your lane and focus on success for you.

12. Remember the power of choice. To *take action* is your choice.

13. Turn in the other direction, if you encounter "Naysayers".

14. Remind yourself *I Got This!*

***

I am ready to release negative self-chatter.

***

Actions I'm Choosing for My Best Self

- I will identify a recurring thought pattern that fills my mind with negative self-chatter. I will replace it with optimistic words and encouragement.

- I will choose to swap my self-doubt with action steps to advance an idea forward.

Chapter 33
Pick Your Passion
and Take Your First Step...

"Find out who you are and be that person.
That's what your soul was put on this earth to be.
Find that truth, live that truth and everything else will come."
— Ellen DeGeneres

Do more of what makes you happy.

Think about the possibilities of what could be.

For this chapter, stretch outside your "box" and look deep into your heart. There is a world of endless possibilities. Just for a moment, reflect on what brings you joy. Not what others want for you, but what is in your heart. In this chapter, we will walk step by step through the process of realizing the passion in your heart. We will start by selecting one of the goals or dreams you have identified during your *Are You Ready?* journey.

Then you will be guided step-by-step on how to realize your passion. Are you ready to choose happier, healthier days and recognize what is sitting in your heart? The next page shows an example as a reference. Then as you move to the following pages, you will create this step-by-step plan for YOU.

Example — Realize Your Passion, Step by Step

This page is an *example of a step-by-step technique.* You will identify the steps to achieve *your dream,* on the next page.

My goal is: Paint a masterpiece to display in an art show.

My first three action steps are:

Step 1: Plan 20 minutes a day to paint my masterpiece.

Step 2: Research and attend local art shows for feedback.

Step 3: Visit an art gallery open house to understand the criteria and requirements to display my artwork.

My target completion dates are:

Step 1: Finish painting my masterpiece on March 21.

Step 2: Exhibit at an art show on April 17.

Step 3: Visit an art gallery open house by May 5.

My fears or obstacles are:

Obstacle 1: I have not painted in many years.

Obstacle 2: No one will like my painting when it is finished.

Obstacle 3: I have no time to paint.

HOW to overcome my fears or obstacles:

Overcoming Obstacle 1: I will buy a canvas and paint supplies. I love to paint and will start enjoying it.

Overcoming Obstacle 2: I will consult with the art gallery for a support contact or classes for guidance on my design.

Overcoming Obstacle 3: I will make myself a priority and paint for 10 to 20 minutes a day for 3 to 5 days each week.

Now, it is your turn to write down your ONE goal or dream. Together, we will create a simple step-by-step plan to help you achieve what has been sitting in your heart.

1 Identify a Goal

My goal is:
(You can also select a goal that you identified in a previous chapter.)

_____

_____

2 Determine the First Three Action Steps

What are the first three action steps to advance you toward your goal? One step at a time at your own pace.

My first three action steps are:

Step 1: _____

Step 2: _____

Step 3: _____

3 Target Completion Date — Timeline

Choose a date to accomplish each of the first three steps. It can be a specific date, such as "May 16 is an art show" or it can be broader, such as "before June 1." Be as specific as possible. After you accomplish your first three action steps, you can repeat the process for your next three steps and so on to reach your goal.

My target completion dates are:

Step 1 complete by: _____

Step 2 complete by: _____

Step 3 complete by: _____

4 Identify Your Barriers

Next, identify the barriers or fears preventing you from reaching your specific goal. As you encounter obstacles, you must become comfortable identifying them, candidly admitting they exist, writing them down, and creating steps on how to overcome them.

My fears or barriers are:

Barrier 1: _____

Barrier 2: _____

Barrier 3: _____

5 HOW to Overcome Obstacles

Often you may suppress your fears, thinking if you do not acknowledge them, they may not exist. The opposite is true — when you identify and write down each fear, then address each one head on, you can overcome them, allowing newfound clarity and focus.

By spotlighting your fears, you can conquer and move past them.

Alright, let's look at how you can plan to *overcome each one of your obstacles* and fears. Here is a step-by-step strategy to leap over your fears. Again, once the first step is completed, then add the next step to overcome your obstacle. This first one is to get you started.

The first step to overcome my obstacles:

First Step – HOW to Overcome Obstacle 1:

_____

_____

First Step – HOW to Overcome Obstacle 2:

_____

_____

First Step – HOW to Overcome Obstacle 3:

_____

_____

6 Schedule Your Steps

It's your turn to schedule each of these action steps on your calendar and or *Me List*. Remember this is for YOU and your future. Focus on what makes you happy and brings you joy.

7 Visualize

What does success look like to you? Create a picture in your mind and on a vision board of you achieving success. Include as many specific details that will capture and bring your achievement to life.

Remember to see yourself welcoming success. To get you started, draw what your success will look like to you.

Here is how I visualize my success:

***

I am ready to focus on one step at a time to realize my passion.

***

Actions I'm Choosing for My Best Self

- I will pick my passion.

- I will identify and accomplish the first three steps, then three more steps until I reach my goal.

- I will display a picture of myself achieving my goal.

Part Five Take-Aways
HOW to Get There
*Simple treasures to nudge you on your journey
to becoming the best version of yourself.*

- Do more of what makes you happy.

- Pick one passion, create the first steps, develop the timeline, and advance your passion forward.

- Schedule your action steps on your calendar.

- *Take the first step even if you cannot see the whole staircase.*

- Advance inch by inch toward your goal.

- Celebrate each step because you <u>are</u> enough.

- Swap your thoughts with action if self-doubt seeps in.

- Step in the other direction if you encounter people who try to make you feel inferior or squash your dreams.

- Stick your neck out to succeed.

- Remember you can handle what is given to you—embrace the thought of success.

- Visualize success.

Part Six

The Whole You
Your Purpose and Brand

Part Six: Introduction
The Whole You
Your Purpose and Brand

You'll learn how to:

❖ Remember your happiness is right inside you.

❖ Discover your true purpose.

❖ Learn what you love that is sitting in your heart.

❖ Make a positive difference doing what you love.

❖ Define the value you bring to the world *today*.

❖ Polish your personal brand.

❖ Be ready to promote yourself.

❖ Create the *Story of You*.

❖ Share the best version of you with others each day.

❖ Be ready to see yourself shine!

Jackie Cantoni

Chapter 34
Your Purpose

"Have the courage to follow your heart and intuition.
They somehow know what you want to become."
— Steve Jobs

We want to make a difference. We crave it. We aspire to bring value to our life and define our purpose. Why are we here? As with many things, can we sometimes overcomplicate our true purpose?

Reflect for a minute. Could your purpose be to become the best version of who you are? If you were to look back on your life and accomplishments so far and compare them to who you think you could still become — namely the best version of you—are they both the same person?

Your purpose can be simple and does not have to be mystical. For me, I find purpose in mentoring. Mentoring is not complex; it is making a positive difference in the lives of others, one person at a time.

"The meaning of life is to find your gift.
The purpose of life is to give it away."
— William Shakespeare

One of the best strategies for discovering your life's purpose is to identify what you love and the value you bring **today.** Purpose is taking the best version of you in each area of your life and sharing that with the world each day, inch by inch. It's when you attempt to determine your entire life's purpose that you can get overwhelmed. Think of purpose as one day at a time. Each day ask yourself, *"What is my purpose for today?"* Then sprinkle this into your daily life.

On some days, your purpose — and being the best version of you — is taking care of and rejuvenating yourself. Purpose can be choosing *Me Time* and enjoying one of your passions. If you are run down, no one benefits, including you. Take care of you. Then you can share your gifts each day with the world. One day at a time.

Alright, let's focus on you. It's your turn to get your creative juices flowing as you think of your daily purpose . . .

1 What do you love to do? What sits in your heart?

_____

_____

_____

2 What are you good at and can share with others?

_____

_____

_____

3 *How can you link one of your passions to a purpose and make a positive difference for others or yourself?* (For example, if you love golf, can you link your passion to teaching golf or volunteering to share your skill with special needs children or senior citizens?) A purpose can be intertwined with your other daily responsibilities.

_____

_____

_____

4 *The First Step to Your True Purpose:*
Reflect on your three answers above and bring them together. What is the first step to move you toward your purpose for today?

_____

_____

_____

Purpose can change over time. Purpose is sharing you, what you love, and your best self with the world each day. Focus on one day at a time — this is your first simple step. Keep in mind, the simple things can make a big difference in creating a happier, healthier life. Some days it can be taking care of others as a parent or caregiver. Some days it may be working to financially provide for your family or your future. At times, it can be finding what you love and then volunteering to give it back to others.

Finding your true purpose can help you create new opportunities, discover your untapped potential, and uncover what has been sitting dormant in your heart. Then like a seedling, it is ready to burst out of the soil and grow.

Alright, it's your turn to tell yourself, *"Today I choose to take the first step toward living my true purpose (as identified in step 4 above). I will take one step at a time to move me closer to the true purpose and passion that sit in my heart."*

And always remember, on some days, your purpose may be rejuvenating and taking care of YOU!

***

I am ready to live my purpose, one day at a time.

***

Actions I'm Choosing for My Best Self

- I will discover what I enjoy and can share with others.

- I will let my purpose, on some days, be taking care of and rejuvenating me.

- I will be the best version of myself and share that with the world each day.

Chapter 35
Making a Difference is Not Always Easy

"If we all did the things we are capable of,
we would literally astound ourselves."
— Thomas Edison

I love to mentor. It is a passion. For living my passion, an inner-city school gave me a Mentor of the Year Award for a Business Connections Program. I didn't even know they had such a recognition — I just did what I enjoyed. I love to coach and make a positive difference in others' lives. But fulfilling this passion didn't come without a few bumps in the road. There were challenges.

My mentoring story began on a Thursday afternoon. I was excited to begin my first hour of a new tutoring and mentoring program. The thought of making a positive difference was just the right motivation for me. Up until then, it rested inactive in my heart.

The subject was Algebra. I thought this was going to be easy since I have some background in math and an MBA in finance. How hard could it be? Yet, each night before the tutoring session, I would open the high school lesson plan and study "how to find x" again. I, too, needed a refresher.

When I arrived at the school, I sat down between two high school juniors. I'll call them Meg and Lisa. The girl on my left, Meg, opened her Algebra book and showed me what she had for homework. We talked about how she would solve the problems and she started her homework. Then I turned to Lisa and asked if she had any questions on her homework. Lisa replied, *"We did not have any homework. I do not need any help."* Before Lisa even finished her sentence, Meg, who only a moment before was working on her homework, closed her book. Meg put the worksheet away and said, "Oh, that's right, we don't have any homework and I don't need any help." Lisa did not want to learn that day and, as a result of peer pressure, her behavior influenced the student who was ready to learn. This happened in a matter of seconds and I thought to myself, "What just happened — what now?!"

As a new mentor, it was truly disheartening. My excitement was replaced with discouragement. I wondered if I was cut out for this, even though I knew deep in my heart I wanted to mentor.

At times, we can get discouraged or fearful we are not qualified for an experience. As easy as it could have been to choose not to return the next week, I gratefully went back each week. Five years later, I was still mentoring.

I learned making a difference is not always easy. However, if it is something I truly want in my heart, I will find ways to overcome the obstacles.

The program director, other mentors, and I worked to create a new one-on-one mentoring approach that was much broader in scope to help the mentees. I enjoyed watching these young ladies succeed. As the program progressed, the students and their mentors made great strides together, each learning from the other. The students I met were bright and talented individuals who just needed a little guidance and a nudge, like most of us. I am thankful I did not let my initial challenges cause me to give up the first day. I learned persistence can create happiness and purpose.

This anonymous happiness quote on my desk reminds me to follow what is in my heart:

> *There is no key to happiness . . . the door is always open.*

For you, as you fulfill your purpose, remember the strategies in *Are You Ready?* to pull you through on certain days. Making a difference is not always easy. Yet, if your passion bubbles out of your heart, you can take a deep breath, say *I Got This!* and bring your gifts to the world.

***

I am ready to realize making a difference is not always easy.

***

Actions I'm Choosing for My Best Self

- I will remember making a difference is not always easy.
- I will choose to overcome my obstacles and share my talents and gifts with the world.

Chapter 36
Promoting You and Your Brand

"Your brand is what people say about you
when you are not in the room."
— Jeff Bezos, Founder of Amazon

Let's explore you and your personal brand.

Take a moment to reflect on a past interview, presentation, or conversation with a new friend. How did you portray yourself? Were you confident and self-assured? Did you recognize your uniqueness and the value you bring to others?

YOU are your brand. How you portray or promote yourself is part of your personal brand. When you think about it, you really are the CEO and president of company YOU. As with any company, the *image* you present, the *mission* you adhere to, the *ideals* for which you stand, and your *vision* that is your driving force all fit into the guidelines the world needs to see and learn about for you to be successful in achieving your goals.

A well-defined and polished personal brand can favorably influence your outcomes whether you are looking for career advancement, speaking in front of an audience, or building a personal or professional relationship.

Your personal brand follows you wherever you go and sometimes even lingers behind when you leave a room.

Your brand, passion, and purpose are connected, although each one is a view through a different lens. Your personal brand is your foundation. It helps promote you in very powerful ways.

Here are three ingredients to focus on as you prepare to confidently promote you and your brand:

1) **You**—identify you.

2) **Your Uniqueness**—discover your unique gifts.

3) **The Value You Bring**—learn the value you bring to others.

1) You

Throughout *Are You Ready?* you had the opportunity to identify a passion. Passion is a defining quality. What could you do or talk about passionately and continuously if someone were there to listen to you? We tend to be more comfortable talking about what we love. Which is another reason why loving yourself is so important.

Let's identify YOU!

What could you do for hours as a labor of love? (This can be your purpose and passion you wrote about in earlier chapters.)

_____

_____

_____

What are your skillsets and strengths?

_____

_____

_____

What are your values? (Note what characteristics and values are important to you. For example, integrity, positive attitude, persistence, and kindness.)

_____

_____

_____

What is your style? (Note the energy and effect you want to present to others. For example, being conservative, out-spoken, professional, entertaining, passionate, funny, and supportive.)

_____

_____

_____

2) Your Uniqueness

Steve Jobs, co-founder of Apple, so aptly explained uniqueness:

"You can't look at the competition and say you are going to do it better. You have to look at the competition and say you are doing it differently."

How are you unique and different from others?

_____

_____

_____

_____

3) The Value You Bring

What problem do you solve or what value do you bring to others? How do you transform their current experience or make their life easier? Think about if you are interviewing, presenting yourself to others, selling a product, or participating in a new activity or sport and you want to let your value shine.

_____

_____

_____

_____

Put Your Three Ingredients Together

These three ingredients — *You, Your Uniqueness, and the Value You Bring* — can help you package yourself and your brand to attract opportunities. Let's pull together what you wrote above for your personal brand and summarize them below. You will then take this vision into the next chapter as your foundation for your *Story of You*.

To summarize:

When I think about my personal brand, I am . . .

_____

_____

_____

When I think of my personal brand, I value . . .

_____

_____

_____

When I think of my personal brand, I bring/offer ...

_____

_____

_____

This reflection is your first step as you think about your uniqueness, talents, and value. As you refine what you stand for — as your personal brand — practice sharing it with a few trusted friends. Be open to making improvements over time. Then, as the CEO of company YOU, you can confidently present yourself and your unique value to the world. You can be guided to stay loyal to yourself as you network with co-workers, business prospects, or even new friends.

Be who you are, not what you think others want you to be. Remember, be authentic. Be you.

***

I am ready to let my uniqueness stand out in the crowd.

***

Actions I'm Choosing for My Best Self

- I will define my brand, uniqueness, and the value I bring to others.

- I will realize building my brand is a journey.

- I will let my personal brand shine through when presenting myself to others, meeting new friends, and living my best life.

Chapter 37
The Story of You

"One of the hardest things in life is to be brave enough to be yourself."
—Lady Gaga

If I asked you, *"Tell me about yourself,"* could you clearly and concisely share you and your uniqueness?

The answer to this question is your value story. A value story builds on your personal brand and succinctly communicates a summary of YOU.

Let's call this value story . . . the *Story of You.*

You might have heard of an elevator pitch. If you were riding in an elevator with a potential client, investor, or future boss, what would you share about yourself that would be an impactful message, moving them to want to know more about what you can offer them? How about your next interview when asked, "Why should we choose you?"

Instead of having to think on your feet for this opportunity of a lifetime, *plan in advance* so you can be *prepared in advance.* You will need to quickly and concisely convey your most important points. Many times, you may only have less than a minute to relay your message. What would you say? What are you seeking to accomplish? How will you capture their attention and make them want to hear more?

Alright, now you can create your elevator pitch — the *Story of You*. Let's get started with the four self-reflections below. Consider your responses from the personal brand chapter, as your brand is a foundation for these answers. Your personal brand already includes the value you will bring to the table and how you are unique.

Here you go . . .

1 How I identify myself:

I am . . .

_____

_____

_____

2 What I offer:

I offer . . .

_____

_____

_____

3 Why should you choose me?

The benefit I bring to my clients, boss, coach, or audience . . .

_____

_____

_____

_____

_____

4 My target client or audience:

My best type of client or audience . . .

_____

_____

_____

_____

_____

Connecting the Dots of YOU

Are you ready for a new opportunity when it knocks on your door? Below, connect the dots from your four reflections to create a powerful, succinct message ready to go in an instant.

Your thoughts may rapidly flow or trickle out. Either way, feel good as you are choosing to create a concise *Story of You*. This is your first step . . .

To get you started and offer guidance, I will share an example of one of my value stories:

> *"I am a mentor and life coach who instills unwavering belief in my mentees, so they clearly see it in themselves. After our discussions, my mentees are inspired with increased self-confidence, focus, and rejuvenation. I guide them step-by-step to discover and celebrate their uniqueness, let go of negative self-chatter, believe in themselves, and uncover their passion to propel forward and toward success.*
>
> *My ideal clients are seeking to be the best version of themselves."*

Alright, now it is your turn . . .

The Story of You

Let's create The Story of You. This is a valuable starting point for presenting or promoting you.

Summarize your thoughts from the four reflections above. Think about if I asked you to *tell me about yourself or why should I consider you for this opportunity?*

_____

_____

_____

_____

_____

_____

_____

_____

_____

_____

_____

_____

Congratulations . . . give yourself a high-five! Your *Story of You* is now getting ready to be packed for your journey. As your next step, plan to practice and review your story with a family member, friend, or mentor to receive feedback on how to tweak or enhance your pitch. This initial outline is your first milestone. You are on your way. Celebrate and recognize your uniqueness as you continue to create the *Story of You.*

You can now stand out amongst the crowd on your journey to your best self. Be ready to see yourself shine!

***

I am ready to share the "Story of Me."

***

Actions I'm Choosing for My Best Self

- I will bring together my true purpose, passion, and brand to create the *Story of Me.*

- I will be prepared when asked, *"Tell me about yourself."*

- I will share the *Story of Me* when interviewing, presenting, promoting myself, or building relationships.

Part Six Take-Aways
The Whole You
Your Purpose and Brand
*Simple treasures to nudge you on your journey
to becoming the best version of yourself.*

- Your purpose is taking the best version of you in each area of your life and sharing that each day.

- Your purpose on some days is also taking care of and rejuvenating you.

- Your personal brand follows you wherever you go and sometimes even lingers behind when you leave a room.

- Your well-defined personal brand can promote you in very powerful ways.

- Your value story is a concise, impactful summary of YOU.

- Your uniqueness is the value you bring to the world.

- Your *Story of You* is packed and ready to go on your journey to your best self.

- Your happiness is right inside you. Remember *"There is no key to happiness . . . the door is always open."*

Are You Ready?

Part Seven

Bringing It All Together for Your Best Self

Part Seven: Introduction
Bringing It All Together for Your Best Self

❖ Reveal yourself as a masterpiece. The distinguished painting now ready for the art gallery is, metaphorically, YOU.

❖ Choose the message you bring to the world each day. Remember, *"You Rock!"*

❖ Focus on your passions, one step at a time, checking off and celebrating each milestone. You may need only a little nudge.

❖ Stay in your lane.

❖ Celebrate because you <u>are</u> enough.

❖ Take the first step — in the direction of your dreams — and your second step will follow.

❖ Move forward with confidence as you encounter people who try to make you feel inferior.

❖ Create memories and a legacy, take care of your financial well-being, and treasure your relationships.

❖ Uncover your true purpose, let your personal brand shine, and share your uniqueness with the *Story of You.*

❖ Appreciate your inner beauty and belief in yourself.

❖ Remember, you are a beautiful swan and *You Got This!*

Jackie Cantoni

Chapter 38
A Masterpiece

"I've come to believe that each of us has a personal calling
that's as unique as a fingerprint."
— Oprah Winfrey

You are a masterpiece. The distinguished painting now ready for the art gallery is, metaphorically, YOU.

"You are a masterpiece and a work in progress at the same time."

One of my best friends, Veronica, shared the above masterpiece quote with me that has many variations yet similar meanings. Although the author is unknown, its inspiring message flows repeatedly throughout *Are You Ready?* On the journey to your best self, you are both a work in progress and a masterpiece.

Reveal yourself as a masterpiece. You are beautiful, unique, and talented. At the same time, know the best version of you will not always be perfect. And that is okay. Life is not perfect. Do not let time slip away waiting for perfection.

Release the weight of the world associated with *trying* to be perfect. *Choose* to see yourself as a masterpiece and embrace who you are *right now*. Celebrate you each day on your journey to your best self. Choose you. Choose the beautiful and unique YOU!

I am ready to realize I am a unique and beautiful masterpiece.

Chapter 39
Bringing It All Together

"Nothing is impossible; the word itself is I'm possible."
— Audrey Hepburn

Bringing it all together is a summary of our journey together . . .

Are You Ready? equipped you with strategies to believe in yourself, make yourself and your passions a priority, and take care of YOU. It guided you to find your true purpose as you built confidence, became sure of yourself, and discovered your best self. Let this book be a place to come back to during the times when you are insecure or unsure of yourself and need a boost to remember why you love being you!

On your life's journey, you discovered you are an artist and can start your day with a blank canvas. Each day, you get to choose your message, attitude, and outlook. Begin your days with love and laughter. Then embrace your uniqueness and let your daily message reflect the remarkable, unique you. Have the courage to share you and your gifts with the world. Remember, *You Rock!*

Start your day with belief in yourself. Believe in you. This belief is the cornerstone to your best self. Let go of self-doubt and negative self-chatter. One strategy to inspire belief in yourself is to nourish your mind with positive self-affirmations — to *appreciate you*. Remember also to place written inspirational messages throughout your home encouraging optimistic thoughts and gratitude. Be grateful for who you are. Reach deep within your heart and uncover your inner beauty. Seek out encouragement from others who are reassuring and uplifting. Continue to build your self-confidence and self-appreciation as you reflect on your *Top 10 Traits That I Love about Myself.*

Remember to see yourself as a confident, beautiful swan.

Rediscover your dreams as you reflect on *The Best Version of Myself Resume at Age 100.* This reflection can help you realize what you may wish you had pursued when you had the opportunity. It's a reminder to focus on you and your passions. Remember that *you matter and to make yourself a priority.* Place *"you"* at the top of your *Me List.* Pick you and take care of yourself daily to re-energize and rejuvenate you.

Choose your best. *Choose* to be the best version of you. You learned to write your *Today I choose to* actions and accomplish your goals through *daily* choices. These choices are about you and your priorities, just for today, one day at a time.

Appreciate the *power of your voice*:

1. Ask for help, support, and guidance.
2. Share your unique blueprint, strengths, and talents.
3. Think and say aloud inspiring self-affirmations.

Remember, sometimes sharing your voice is *listening* to a friend.

On your journey to your best self, the first step can be the most frightening. What are you afraid of? As we discussed, doubt and fear are more likely to squash more dreams than failure from pursuing something new. Believe in yourself and you can accomplish your goals, one step at a time. Identify and overcome one barrier at a time by *asking HOW and planning the action steps.*

The door to your life is wide open, take the first step in and your second step will follow — creating momentum. Become at ease as you stick your neck out like the tortoise. Move through your days at your own pace, surely and steadily, inch by inch.

Do you often compare yourself to others? Eliminate the anxiety associated with the comparison and choose to *stay in your lane.* Shift your focus to yourself and your priorities. *Replace competitive energy with a picture of success for you.*

Quiet your mind to hear what is in your heart. You have it in you. If you are too busy pleasing everyone else, you may never get the opportunity to accomplish what you hold in your heart. You learned to say No! to "I'm so busy" and YES to you and your priorities. *Take care of you and release the guilt.* Saying yes to yourself can result in happier, more fulfilling days.

Build your days with connections and treasure friendships. Disconnect from your devices and reconnect with those around you. Remember why you fell in love with your significant other. Hold hands and look each other in the eyes. Be his or her biggest fan and lift each other up. Relationships are a gift to yourself.

Are You Ready?

Nurture your *relationship with yourself. Remember why you love being you*! Forgive others as well as yourself. Then repurpose this energy and share your joy with those you love, including you.

Pick a day of kindness and keep it to yourself. Do you feel better about yourself when you are kind? Spread kindness and positivity everywhere you go. Begin with a smile. Share your smile. *"When you smile at someone, if they don't smile back, then they needed your smile more than you."* Be grateful daily. Remember gratitude is a key that unlocks the door to a joyful spirit. Embrace gratefulness to boost your attitude. Sprinkle in laughter and release the weight of the world. Plan to laugh . . . belly laugh each day. Have fun being you and sharing you with the world.

Remember, life is your perspective. When you are faced with an inconvenience can you say *So what?* Or when confronted with a challenge or new opportunity, can you release the negative self-chatter or self-doubt and say *I Got This!*

"Practice believing in you. Choose you." Let your light shine.

Focus on *the whole you* and take care of your health and your financial security. Recall your *triggers* and *the why* of your eating pattern as you choose to become a healthier version of yourself. Give attention to your financial well-being. Pay yourself first so you can realize a financial goal or passion. Round out *the whole you* by creating memories and traditions with your loved ones as part of your legacy.

As you journey through each day, you can *pop open* and be contagious with a positive and optimistic attitude. You can bring back childhood creativity, imagination, and understand possibilities are endless.

Discover what you love and reveal it to the world. Your purpose can be taking the best version of you in each area of your life and sharing that each day. You learned making a difference is not always easy. However, if it is important to you, you will find a way to share your gifts with others. Remember, on some days your purpose can be rejuvenating and taking care of yourself.

You are the CEO of YOU and have polished your personal brand. *You discovered your uniqueness, strengths, and the value you bring to others.* You are ready to promote YOU. Now, the next time you come across an opportunity; you can stand out in the crowd with a well-defined, polished *Story of You*.

You are a beautiful masterpiece. Embrace your uniqueness, talent, and inner beauty. Be inspired to sparkle with self-confidence as you *choose* to be the best version of you. *The most important investment you will ever make is in yourself.*

Focus on the *simplicity* of these strategies to help you overcome the *complexity* in your life. Inch by inch and day by day — love and appreciate you.

Be you . . . the best version of you. You Got This!

I am ready to be the best version of myself.

Chapter 40
Pass It On . . .

*"It's not about being unafraid.
It's about being afraid and doing it anyway."*
— author unknown

Pass on your uniqueness and gift to the world.

Why not begin at home or with those you love? You now choose to believe in yourself, and you have the tools and strategies to fulfill your purpose. Can you pay it forward and help a family member or a friend realize his or her passions, set priorities, and discover their personal brand and unique value?

As a parent, a friend, or a leader, one of the best gifts you can give to others is confidence. Confidence to believe in themselves, to appreciate the value they bring to the world, to pursue their passions and strive to be their personal best.

As they walk through *Are You Ready?* like you, help them celebrate their uniqueness, talents, and who they are today.

You can make a difference one person at a time. As you become the best version of yourself, have the confidence to share this gift with others — helping them become the best version of themselves. Pass on the remarkable you to the world. Share the gift of YOU. *You Rock!*

I am ready to pass along the gift of self-belief to others.

Jackie Cantoni

THE END
...Or is it your beginning?

Do You. Be You. Celebrate You.

Notes:

Jackie Cantoni

Notes:

Are You Ready?

Notes:

Made in the USA
Middletown, DE
05 July 2019